CW00550861

Change is hard. It takes
rewards are great. Let *Th*
and timely book.
     —Marshall Goldsmith   *...es vestselling author and*
                 world leading leadership thinker and executive coach.

The first step is the hardest. Yet with each passing step it gets
easier—we understand the journey is for ourselves, our body,
our mind, our overall wellbeing. Steven's book is a critical tool
for that first step, and to remind us everyday, that today is not
the day to stop.

                    —Roberto Di Bernardini,
             Chief Human Resources Officer, Danone

What I love about *The Daily Reset* is that it goes beyond the
standard pushes to do better or more productive things in your
life and into the science behind why those things matter. What a
great way to reset your thinking!

             —Jeff Gothelf, bestselling author of Lean UX,
             Sense & Respond *and* Forever Employable

Every day I look forward to my dose of *The Daily Reset.* I
prepare a coffee and as I read the day's nudge I know I will be
inspired to reflect on what the day will bring. It's now a habit
and I'm proud of it.

            —Rory Simpson, Chief Learning Officer, Telefónica

I'm a huge fan of Steven's approach to improvement and
new ways of working through small, sustainable steps!
The Daily Reset is wonderfully written and a powerful
inspiration for personal change.

            —Tobias Haug, Head of Humanizing Business, SAP

Dr. Steven MacGregor is the Founder of The Leadership Academy of Barcelona, Honorary Professor of Health and Wellbeing at the Glasgow School of Art, and External Advisor for McKinsey & Company. Across a 20-year career in wellbeing, he has helped improve the workplace health and sustainable leadership of tens of thousands of professionals worldwide at organisations including Salesforce, Santander, and Telefónica. His previous books include *Sustaining Executive Performance* and *Chief Wellbeing Officer*, which is also a podcast. A former national Duathlon Champion (triathlon for bad swimmers) he has trained with Olympic track athletes, Tour de France cyclists, and Ironman champions. He lives in Barcelona with his wife Pamela, son Matthew, and sheepdog Teddy.

www.stevenmacgregor.com
hello@stevenmacgregor.com
🐦 @spmacg
📷 @spmacg
🔗 Dr. Steven MacGregor

THE
DAILY
RESET

366 NUDGES TO MOVE YOUR LIFE FORWARD

STEVEN P. MACGREGOR

AUTHOR OF *CHIEF WELLBEING OFFICER*
AND *SUSTAINING EXECUTIVE PERFORMANCE*

Edited by Kerry Parke
Cover design by Ferran Bruguera
Interior design & typesetting by Jennifer Blais
Author photograph by Katie McKie

For information on buying this title in bulk quantities, or for custom editions please email: hello@stevenmacgregor.com.

First published December 2021 by Sheepdog Press.
ISBN 10:84-09-34252-9
ISBN 13:978-84-09-34252-5

Registered with the Publishers Guild Federation of Spain.

CONTENTS

*To the people of the town of Motherwell where I grew up,
and the people of the city of Barcelona where I found my voice.*

INTRODUCTION

In the midst of that unforgettable first pandemic lockdown of March 2020, there were two things that kept me going. First, I went back to journaling and ended each day by writing some thoughts down on paper before turning off the light and going to sleep. I have kept a journal on and off for most of my life, starting a diary as a young teenager in order to track my athletic progress and then to salve my growing teenage angst. For me, journaling helps keep me grounded and provides a daily anchor to what truly matters to me amid the maelstrom of life.

Second, I read *The Daily Stoic* by Ryan Holiday and Stephen Hanselman every morning as I prepared coffee. It was maybe the second or third year I had picked up the book but, to be honest, it was the first time that I kept up with the readings and exercises. As I write these words now, almost eighteen months later, that book is still an indispensable part of my morning ritual—*almost* as important as coffee. It has helped me understand the importance of going with the ebb and flow of life, to stop trying to control things and to understand the power and freedom of focusing on my own reasoned choices. For our post-pandemic world, I can't think of a better daily guide, and I hope that my book also helps people return to a less restricted life.

The Daily Reset is at once a journal and a daily coach. Read it, write in it, highlight ideas you think are useful and disagree with those you do not. Above all, *experiment*. In these pages, you will find 366 *nudges*—reflections, questions, hacks, facts, stories, methods, and memories for you to change behaviour for good— to help keep wellbeing and a positive working life top of mind each day of the year.

How should you use *The Daily Reset*? There is a page to read each day of the year, perhaps in the morning or at night. This is one approach. If you prefer to read all the way through regardless of dates or jump to a specific section based on your interest or immediate need, that works too. My only wish is that you *engage*—by writing in the spaces provided or by moving to action and testing out the ideas each day. On some days, there is a clear action or question to answer while others are open to interpretation. Sometimes I'll try and push you, perhaps into a zone of discomfort (where we grow) and on some days, we'll take it easy. This is how we learn. Through increments, pushing at times beyond our current limits and then allowing for a period of recovery before pushing again.

This journal is aimed at improving your health and wellbeing—on all levels. Physical, mental, emotional, spiritual, career, social, anything you can think of and require. As we emerge from the reset of the pandemic, *brain health* may show itself to be particularly relevant. It is an emerging concept that includes neural development and recovery throughout our lives. It therefore not only includes being well, but translating that wellbeing into the right behaviour and choosing to play an active role in the new world.

We all have the opportunity get to write a new page of our lives each and every day. No matter if we have a fabulous day or a terrible one, we go to sleep and reset for the new one ahead. What we do in the future shouldn't be constrained by what happened in the past, even when good. Each daily reset gives us an opportunity to improve by tiny yet valuable margins, and I hope to provide some guidance and inspiration to enable you to do that. It's time to move forward. The pandemic held us in limbo, stuck. As restrictions begin to lift around the world, I sense a growing momentum around being unstuck.

The pandemic also raised the notion of reset the world over. Many called it 'The Great Reset' which links to different ideas, from the much-needed breather for the natural world to our collective questioning of the way we live our lives. Mental health was discussed with particular frequency and many people began to adopt their own measures to reset and protect that most precious resource.

All put together, this concept of reset highlights an opportunity to actively shape the new world—a type of 'building back better'. That starts with re-shaping who we are as individuals. I'm not preaching. My approach to teaching wellbeing over the years has come from an awareness of my own failings and vulnerabilities in life. The 366 nudges that comprise *The Daily Reset* are both *my* journal and *your* journal. I have used, and will continue to use, each and every one. Sometimes, I find—like you might—that I just can't make them work on a given day. I think there's a valuable lesson in that too.

Writing this book in the summer of 2021 marks my twenty-year journey working in the field of wellbeing. In 2001 I was a visiting researcher at Stanford when I started to identify the questions that I'm still trying to answer today. Indeed, we are entering an 'age of wellbeing' where we are finally, *en masse*, asking the important questions about what it means to *be well* in our lives.

Wellbeing is a journey. We might not find the right path the first time. In fact, it's something that is always changing, evolving as we adapt to the way our life journey throws us surprises, setbacks and fortune, pleasure and pain. Such is the richness of life.

Both journey and journal come from the same root, the Old French *jour*, or day. Every journey starts with a step, a day. If you don't get it right today, simply reset. And go again tomorrow.

Let's begin.

MY RESET START DATE: ....

REFLECTIONS ON WHERE I AM NOW

VISIT WWW.DAILYRESET.ME FOR EXTRA RESOURCES

JANUARY

MOVEMENT

READY? *RESET,* GO!

"I have two doctors, my left leg and my right."
G.M. Trevylan

We move less as we age, and walking is no exception. As well as walking less, we begin to walk *slower*. Research has shown walking speeds to be an accurate marker of mortality, especially for older men, and this goes beyond the expected cardiovascular (heart health) to a wide variety of causes.

With each passing year, which tend to click by at an ever-increasing pace, there are often imperceptible changes in who we are and how we function. Of course, as we accumulate experience along with those passing years, we hope that we become wiser versions of ourselves. Yet, there are a myriad of hidden areas that demand greater attention—on a physical, emotional, spiritual, and other levels. A gentle nudge is all that's required. So, for starters, please keep walking. And keep walking fast.

Pick up the pace today. It's a new year. It's a good day.

HOW MUCH DO YOU MOVE?

L et's get back to basics. Never mind the speed, sometimes we rarely walk at all these days, right?

People walked significantly more in recent history, simply because they had no other choice. In the modern world we have become too clever. We have engineered movement right out of our lives. It is viewed as an inconvenience. Chairs, elevators, cars, 'moving sidewalks' in airports—all are symbols of our sedentary age.

Doctors have a name for the negative health impacts of a highly sedentary life—"sitting disease"—and *Harvard Business Review* picked up on this idea within the context of work citing that 'Sitting is the smoking of our generation'. So, just as we were with tobacco in the mid 20th century, we risk being unaware of the real health dangers of a highly sedentary life, which has also been shown to cut life expectancy at the same level as being a medium to heavy smoker.

At the start of each month, it is worthwhile to check in on where you are on the scale. And if you feel you are ok, great. And what about the people around you? Of course, try to remember, it's about gently raising awareness (not preaching).

WE WERE BORN TO MOVE

S cientists say our ancestors moved up to 12 miles (around 20km) every day.

Why? Perhaps obvious that they did so in order to survive—to either hunt or escape danger. Movement is therefore part of our DNA, part of our survival imperative.

This doesn't mean you have to move 12 miles every day. Indeed, I've said to thousands of people over the years it's better to focus on sitting less in a day than becoming a Marathon runner. Because even regular exercisers are not immune to the effects of sitting disease, the goal of 'sitting less' is a quicker win, one with impact and sustainable change.

Stay true to your human nature today.

MOVEMENT CREATES ENERGY

What's the default response to feeling tired? Sleeping more? A short nap? Lying down? More often than not, it's moving *less,* right? What if you tried moving *more* instead?

Of course, movement requires energy. However, it also *creates* energy. There are different processes at play when we move, including a rising metabolism and the creation of different chemicals in the brain. Psychophysiologist Dr. Charles Hillman has shown that we essentially "switch ourselves on" by moving. Yet the most straightforward reason of all is increased blood flow. Blood carries oxygen and oxygen gives us energy, to our bodies and to our brains.

No doubt there will be several instances today when you feel tired. Check your default response. Instead of moving less, try flipping the script.

BEWARE THE CHAIR (PART I)

There are no chairs in the Bible, or in Shakespeare's *Hamlet*. Yet, *Bleak House* by Charles Dickens, published in the middle of the 19th century has 187 of them. So notes Professor Vybarr Cregan-Reid, author of *Primate Change: How the world we made is remaking us.*

Cregan-Reid traces the fascinating historical evolution of the chair and writes that at one time it would have been of as much use to the peasantry as a crown and was associated, for centuries, with power, wealth, and high status. This idea is still present today. For example, the highest post in a university department is called the 'Chair' while the 'best seat in the house' is often reserved for special guests or VIPS.

The industrial revolution changed everything and as chairs became more necessary and useful, a pattern of human inactivity was set in motion and it has changed our very biology.

Cregan-Reid estimates there to be around 60 billion chairs in the world today.

But that doesn't mean you have to sit in one all day.

SHOW US YOUR DANCE MOVES

'm a terrible dancer. Quite ironic for someone who is married to a trained dancer and choreographer. Dance is a physically demanding pursuit that yields deep gains on both a cardiovascular and strength level, yet it is also filled with emotion.

During the initial months of the pandemic, I reconnected with some special songs from my youth. They immediately transported me back to that time and, before I knew it, some terrible teenage dancing was taking place in my living room.

I don't think it matters how bad you are (and, really, kudos if you are good). More importantly, few other activities connect the body and mind so deeply. Dance to interpret what's going in your head, to improve both physical and mental health.

What's your favourite song?

When was the last time you danced?

After this period in history when we've been told to maintain a safe physical distance from others, dancing with other human beings might, too, satisfy an important need.

STAND-UPS
SAVE TIME

A re you now back into the swing of things at work? The next several days focus on the workplace, so if this doesn't apply to your life right now think on the other spaces you inhabit each day.

If you are working, how are those meetings going?

As a young engineering student, I spent several of my placement summers in a workshop or plant setting. I recall the practice of 'toolbox talks'—short, focused, actionable, and frequent standing huddles of conversation to get the work done.

One of the defining features of the recent agile transformation in workplaces worldwide is the standing meeting. People most often report on the current status of their job, what they're doing that day, and any problems encountered.

Standing meetings are shorter. People are more focused. They allow you to claim back your precious time.

Try implementing it today and write some notes below on how it went.

DESKS ARE NOT
JUST FOR SITTING

The Fourth Industrial Revolution is characterised by different types of work. The global pandemic, in forcing us to work from home and raising the valid question of whether we should even go back to the office, has emphasised the variety of things we do.

Whether individual or collaborative, creative or routine, time-sensitive or exploratory, urgent or important (or indeed both)— all activities can benefit from different and specific body positions.

Why then should we stick with the conventional one-size-fits-all seated desk?

Many modern office furniture companies now provide a height adjustment function to create a standing desk. Yet even if you don't have one, get creative. Use some other object to raise your desk height (I've used my Oxford English Dictionary, among other things) or model yourself after Ernest Hemingway and work on a bookcase or another piece of furniture.

Standing also burns more calories than sitting. Researchers at the University of Chester calculated this to be an extra 50 per hour, which means that if you stand for three to four hours a day at work, it is the equivalent of running ten marathons a year.

Now, you can choose to run those ten marathons a year if you wish...

WALKING
AT WORK

"When I see someone at their desk all day,
it's suspicious how they pretend to work."
David Kelley, IDEO

The First Industrial Revolution was characterised by specialisation of work. People would have their own workstation and do their thing from that place. In the Fourth Industrial Revolution work is so much more. Yet, we find it hard to shake the legacy of a previous age, still believing that work is something one does at a desk and, even more, with their head down.

'Management by Walking Around' is a long-practiced method in which managers raise their awareness of company operations through unstructured wandering. You may not personally have license to roam like this but when you can, take a walk around your workplace. The practice helps increase visibility, awareness, and build relationships.

WALKING TO WORK

T he natural progression from yesterday's reflections is to think about the getting to and from work.

Commuting is a controversial topic that varies greatly around the world. In some places, a commute can add hours to a working day and cause a significant amount of stress, detracting from our wellbeing. Furthermore, many of us work during the commute. According to research from the University of the West of England which analysed commuter routes into London, the working day had been extended on average about two hours thanks to all of those emails sent and received on the way to work.

Enforced working from home during the pandemic was a life-saver (literally and figuratively) for millions, yet there were many who actually missed the commute. The daily structure of getting to work and home can serve as an important transition ritual that creates a valuable buffer between work and home. For most, jumping out of bed and straight onto the laptop can be rather abrupt.

The hybrid future that is in store for many requires us to be more intentional about our work commute.

Whether you are working from home or in the office, some movement at the beginning and end of your working day can serve as breathing space and has a range of benefits.

What would that look like for you and how might you build it in?

ZOOM FATIGUE

The pandemic increased our awareness about daily ways of working. This has been a benefit. However, the jump to virtual has also exacerbated the typical office sedentary life. Instead of those short walks from our desk to the meeting room, we often found ourselves in back-to-back and endless Zooms.

Virtual meeting fatigue is real and comes from a variety of factors, including the extra work our brains need to do to fill in the missing background information we would pick up during a face-to-face encounter. Recent research from Jeremy N. Bailenson also shows that looking at our own image for an excessive amount of time is emotionally draining.

So, it's important to combat virtual meeting fatigue (because, let's be honest, it looks like the Zoom meetings are here to stay). The simplest method of all may be what was concluded from Microsoft research that looked at the negative impact of back-to-back meetings:

Take a short break.

Better still, move a little before the next one.

DON'T WAIT FOR A FIRE TO TAKE THE STAIRS

Volkswagen created a popular series of 'fun theory' video shorts a few years ago; one of those was 'piano stairs', where they built a piano on a set of subway stairs in Stockholm, resulting in a 66% increase in people taking the stairs instead of the escalator.

Subway stairs are a common focus in studies related to improving citizen health, and building design may be another. Why is the elevator often the first thing we see when entering a building instead of the staircase? Even finding the staircase in many modern-day buildings, especially hotels, is a tough task. An opportunity for movement, and the associated benefits of heart health and weight management, is missed.

Even using the stairs is not permitted in certain companies that are afraid of accidents in the stairway—this is 'health and safety' with a narrow, short-term view.

Taking the stairs doesn't just benefit you in the physical sense, it also gives you a mental break. You won't be checking your phone as much or replying to emails when walking up the stairs as you would in the elevator.

In case of fire, of course, take the stairs, but don't wait on a fire to take the stairs.

MAKE YOUR DAY HARDER

I n my talks over the past few years, I've shown a video from Canadian medical practitioner Dr. Michael Evans called *Let's Make Our Day Harder*. It's worth a watch the next time you're online.

In the video, Evans takes aim at our societal attitudes towards movement and the dangers of a sedentary life or 'sitting disease'. It is a powerful call to action, which makes you think differently about your everyday choices.

We are encouraged to look at the 'hard things'—physical labour and activities as opportunities rather than inconveniences. Exercise therefore doesn't need to be dedicated time set aside from your busy day—it can be the means by which you live your life, every day.

The world around us is the best gym we could possibly design. So, it comes down to your choices. Use the world's gym today.

CREATE A MOVEMENT

You may now be committed to taking the stairs instead of the elevator whenever the opportunity presents itself. Yet, it's not always so easy, especially when social behaviour comes into play. For example, you find yourself in conversation with a colleague at work and they automatically take the elevator. You are likely to follow their lead—after all there's a conversation to finish.

Take a look around you today or the next time you're in the office. You're likely to spot a number of sedentary habits that enforce an unhealthy culture. But, remember, it only takes one person to create *a movement of movement*. A more positive culture where work, and especially quality work, doesn't mean sedentary office time where everyone complains about how busy they are. Set an example that others find inspiring and easy to copy.

Do something different today.

Stick with it.

Others will follow.

MOVING FORWARD

S tarting *The Daily Reset* was a daunting prospect. Writing 366 reflections was intimidating. The finish line seemed so far away, but I found that the monthly themes helped. Studies show that breaking down a big goal into chunks can help you keep moving forward.

And I looked for progress in any dimension. Number of words was a useful early proxy. Getting past 5,000 after the first ten days seemed a big deal (the overall length of *The Daily Reset* is 64,000 words) though at certain times good progress only meant 5,000 words per day. Some days it was nothing to do with words but finishing a draft of a full month. On others it was simply a single idea.

Progress fuelled my long journey. And the nature of progress changes over time. In fact, regress is often the more natural phenomena as time passes. Let me give you an example.

Olympic Champion cyclist Chris Hoy naturally became slower in pure sprinting terms towards the end of his career. Yet he looked for personal bests in other areas, such as leg strength, which ensured he remained competitive. So, look for progress along any measure, not just the obvious ones. Tracking or measuring helps us find and be more mindful of progress which, in turn, acts as fuel for continuing the tracking, and the practice.

The pandemic resulted in many of us becoming stuck. It's time now to move forward. In which area of your life do you need progress?

WALK AND TALK

W hy do we follow the orthodoxy of a meeting where we sit across from one another at a desk? To begin with, it's quite an adversarial positioning. In a walking meeting, both people have the same view, which often helps with reaching a shared understanding. It can also help reduce the pressure around a sensitive topic.

A well-known advocate of the walk and talk, Steve Jobs believed in the value of getting to know someone on a walk and often used the tactic during recruitment and for drilling down on a tough problem.

Instead of booking a meeting room, ask someone if they'd like to go for a walk. In my experience, they're likely to be surprised, but unlikely to refuse.

How did it go?

If you've met this person before, note down any differences in the dynamics of the conversation or your rapport.

IT'S CALLED A MOBILE PHONE

You're working at home, but that doesn't mean you can't implement the same logic around movement as you did when at the office.

Take your device and leave the desk. Cut the video feed on virtual meetings and focus on the conversation. Walk around your home office. Walk around your home. Walk around the garden. Walk around the neighbourhood.

You'll be amazed at how it helps you think more clearly.

TIME TO THINK

n *Harvard Business Review*, American entrepreneur and activist Dan Pallotta explained going for a walk but not calling it a break, citing his own preparation for an important assignment that required hard focus and a type of thinking that progressed much more rapidly during the process of walking.

The office (or home office) is often beset by distractions, so heading out for a walk is often the best means of getting stuff done. And thinking is one of the most important tasks we're engaged in.

Remember that the next time someone gives you a hard time for heading out for a walk. Even yourself.

WALKING AND CREATIVITY

"All truly great thoughts are conceived
by walking."

Friedrich Nietzsche

Walking has been employed by some of history's best thinkers and creative geniuses. Countless writers from Jean-Jacques Rousseau, to William Blake and Wordsworth all used walking to tap into their creativity.

Researchers from the Faculty of Education at Stanford University have also looked at the creative benefit of walking. They found that walking indoors or outdoors similarly boosted creative inspiration—the act of walking itself, and not the environment, was the main factor. Across the board, creativity levels were consistently and significantly higher for those walking compared to those sitting. A person walking indoors—on a treadmill in a room facing a blank wall—or walking outdoors in the fresh air produced twice as many creative responses compared to a person sitting down, with the increased creativity evident during the walk and shortly afterwards.

Struggling to get traction on a problem? Go for a walk and see what happens.

EMBODIED COGNITION THEORY

How we feel mentally and emotionally affects how we act physically. I think we all understand that. If you are tired, sad, or experiencing some other inner state it will have an effect on your physical self.

The opposite is also true, that how we physically act affects our mental and emotional states. A well-known experiment focused on the act of smiling. One group of participants were given chopsticks to hold in their mouths in a way that forced them to mimic a smile. The results showed this to be the happiest group—yet they weren't *really* smiling, only adopting the physical act of smiling.

If you're slouching at your desk, you're telling your mind that you feel powerless.

As Jordan Peterson notes in his first rule of *12 Rules for Life*, 'Stand up straight with your shoulders back'.

TURTLE TEXTING

I have learned a lot from seeing my wife train and work as a dancer, as well as spending time with her dancing friends. Dancers know how to hold their body—they have great posture which often lasts throughout their life.

Many of us, though, have terrible posture and this is the result of two specific tendencies.

Long hours sitting at a desk without taking a break result in an increased hunched position. As well as the powerlessness noted in yesterday's nudge, this hunch creates a greater compressive force on our lumbar spine which can cause permanent deterioration of our discs. Rounded shoulders also decrease the volume of the chest and lungs, which mean we breathe less air and, in turn, feel less alert.

The other culprit is our mobile device, the use of which—even when standing—often results in us craning our necks downwards resulting in an increased load on our spinal column. The greater the angle of lean, the greater the force. Sometimes called 'text neck' this can result in short-term symptoms including severe headaches and chronic issues such as spinal degeneration.

Some studies have created an image of what the typical person may look like in the future given these types of habits. Once you see that image, you'll never again forget the importance of posture.

BEWARE THE CHAIR
(PART II)

Stanford Design School research looked at the different ways we sit and how this affects a common creativity method, that of brainstorming.

What they found is that the design of the chair affect peoples' behaviour in regards to their criticism of other ideas.

One of the key rules of brainstorming is that we build on the ideas of others, even the wild and unrealistic ones, in order to construct a point of departure that might result in a more feasible, innovative idea. The researchers found that when people were sitting on comfortable sofa-type chairs, resting back, they would criticize the ideas of others and the sessions wouldn't go so well. When the comfortable chairs were replaced with more uncomfortable stools, the brainstorm participants—perched on the edge of their seats—actually tended to support more ideas and the overall creative process improved.

Along similar lines, the link between posture and defensiveness has been investigated by researchers at the Olin Business School. Comparing the work of groups with a table and chairs to those without, the study found that those who remained standing were less territorial, more collaborative, and more excited about their work.

As we discussed earlier this month, there are billions of chairs in the world today, but that doesn't mean you have to sit in one all day.

AROUND THE WATER-COOLER

O ne of the big misses from office life during the pandemic was the accidental encounters in the hallway and around the coffee machine that led to cross-fertilisation of ideas and boosted innovation. These serendipitous meetings are almost impossible to re-create online and are one of the factors that will ensure we go back to the office in some shape or form.

The office we do return to will likely be adapted to better suit our varying needs. Let's play an active role in that transformation.

- Go see someone at their desk instead of calling or emailing.
- Try moving the coffee machine or office printer to encourage people to move more.
- Move desks and meeting areas near a large window so people get more natural daylight.

WHAT ELSE COULD YOU DO?

WALKING IS MAKING A COMEBACK

"I'd rather cry in the back of a BMW than smile on a bicycle."

Chinese game show contestant, Ma Nuo

A rtist Karl Jilg created a powerful illustration for the Swedish Road Administration which shows the space that modern society has given to the car. He replaced all roads with a cavernous drop and positioned citizens along the edge in order to create an immediate emotional reaction that spotlights the choices we have made.

In many aspects, the pandemic has served as a time machine, one that has accelerated changes already in motion, particularly in urban design, such as generally less space for cars and more space for walking, buses and bicycles.

Walking made a comeback during the pandemic. If the trend continues, which hopefully it does, we may stroll around the urban spaces of the future and look back puzzled at our 20th century choices.

THE 15-MINUTE CITY

My wife and I, like millions of other families I'm sure, discussed at length during the early stages of the pandemic if we should leave the city. With everyone working from home, why shouldn't we enjoy more space closer to nature? The high cost of living in the city just didn't seem worth it.

The concept of the 15-minute city might just keep people where they are, and for good reason. Developed by Professor Carlos Moreno at the Sorbonne in Paris, the concept of "la ville du quart d'heure" is one in which daily urban necessities are within a 15-minute reach on foot or by bike. Work, home, shops, entertainment, education, and healthcare should all be available—in Moreno's vision—within the same time a commuter might once have waited on a railway platform.

Attempts at implementation of the 15-minute city have been made in Paris, Glasgow, and Portland, with people describing it as a return to a local way of life.

Many cities around the world were first created by a number of small neighbourhoods which joined together, Barcelona included. Are we going back to go forwards? Will it be enough to keep you happy in the city?

THE TYRANNY OF CONVENIENCE

"The Tyranny of Convenience" is an opinion article published in 2018 in *The New York Times* by Columbia University professor of law Tim Wu.

Wu argues that we've made our lives more convenient in many ways but this hasn't made our lives better—or, at least, that the convenience is not in our best interests.

When we rage or become impatient with the WiFi not working, waiting in a long queue, or the slow elevator, we're showing our addiction for convenience and how we are moving along a path that leads to the type of dysfunctional human experience depicted in the Pixar animation *Wall·E*.

Convenience plays an important role in our lives. In fact, the 15-minute city reflected on yesterday could be a case in point, yet if taken too far, we could end up moving less, thinking less, choosing to take the easy option. And this isn't good for our wellbeing. We sometimes need to the do the hard thing, to stretch ourselves. That is the optimum human experience.

Ask yourself today if you might benefit from a little more inconvenience (the good kind).

Maybe the way you move through your day will be a part of that.

THE CELEBRATED CAPTAIN BARCLAY

Accusations of performance-enhancing drugs, riots at an overcrowded Madison Square Garden to watch sports celebrities do battle, professional gambling on a massive scale, and dirty tricks campaigns. Welcome to the 1870s and the world of competitive walking. Pedestrianism was the world's first popular spectator sport in which athletes would often walk distances of up to 500 miles and more around loops of a dirt track in front of sold-out arenas. And the sporting fervour can be traced to one man.

Robert Barclay Allardice, a Scottish soldier, walked 1,000 miles in 1,000 hours for 1,000 guineas—a professional bet that captured the attention of all of Britain. A mile walked every hour, day and night, for almost six weeks. With no more than 40 minutes uninterrupted sleep during all that time, he would start at ten minutes to the hour and, walking briskly, he could finish before the hour struck, then continue for a further mile in the first ten minutes of the next hour. The total amount of side bets was astronomical, some €50M in today's money.

A historic celebration of walking.

If you baulk at the prospect of walking one mile today, preferring instead to drive, perhaps it's time to think a little differently.

YIN AND YANG

At its best, movement helps our minds as much as our bodies.

Remaining curious and open throughout your life to the many ways you can move your body will keep you both physically and mentally healthy, especially since ageing results—there's no way around it—in a natural deterioration of our physical selves. This doesn't just include physical strength but also arguably more important facets such as balance and coordination.

In certain cultures, movement is a philosophy which combines the physical and mental, even spiritual. Yoga from India and Capoeira from Brazil are two examples. Qi Gong from China is another. In Chinese medicine our health, and life in general, is about the balance between Yin and Yang. Yin is quiet, still, and restorative. Yang is loud, expressive, and bold. Qi Gong introduces more of that much needed Yin into the lives of its practitioners—through slowing the breath and stretching muscles and tendons, extending range of movement.

Make plans to explore new forms of movement today and invest in your present and future self. Consider whether you need more Yin or Yang and try to find a balance.

MOVEMENT CULTURE

An influential movement teacher, Ido Portal has attempted to combine the wide variety of movement disciplines that exist—from dance to yoga, martial arts to athletics—and create a 'movement culture' to connect and therefore understand the different types of *movers*, whether they move for physical health or artistic expression.

The movement examples of Portal and the people around the world who follow his approach can be striking, sometimes even uncomfortable to watch. The focus is on dynamic movement as opposed to the isolated development of one part of the body. Actions such as crawling, doing a handstand, and balancing a stick vertically on one's hand all make you think differently about movement and see it for the incredible depth of possibility that it contains.

Try moving in a way today that you've never previously done. Think about how this change in movement affects the way you think, feel, and act throughout your day.

LEARNING TO MOVE

L earning to move is one of the greatest accomplishments of our early lives.

As babies we start to crawl between six and eleven months while our first unassisted steps typically come between eight and eighteen months. This development is aided by practice, and failure. Research published in 2012 in *Psychological Science* found a group of twelve to nineteen-month-olds averaged 2,368 steps per day, and falling 17 times/hour.

At University, movement is celebrated as a key part of the learning culture—a means of continuing our human development. In old age too it is celebrated—a means of pushing back on ageing and also enjoying the greater flexibility people enjoy.

During many other times of our lives, however, it is pushed out and relegated to snatched moments in the evening or during the weekend once more important things are done.

Today, ask yourself if you need to continue your learning journey with movement. Or indeed, what you need to re-learn.

Here's a simple, concrete example to try right now—can you do a squat? (Sit down on your haunches, heels flat on the ground.) Billions do this every day in Asia—which benefits spinal health—but surprisingly few can do it in the West without falling over!

KEEP EXPLORING

Every new day offers us an opportunity to move again.

And I think it helps tremendously if we also move along another path. I mean this literally. A new route allows us to see new things, learn, adopt a different perspective and add distinctness, zest and freshness to our lives should that be required.

If you plan to move today—by whatever means, walking, cycling, running, driving, flying—simply take a path that you've never moved along before.

And keep your eyes open. You may be surprised what happens.

NOTES ON YOUR JOURNEY THROUGH
MOVEMENT IN JANUARY:

FEBRUARY

HABITS

TIME TO CHANGE FOR REAL

[MY JOURNAL]

How did your New Year resolutions go? If you worked through *The Daily Reset* during the month of January, I hope you experienced some change regarding how you move. But, let's be realistic, New Year resolutions usually fail. How did the people around you fare?

The month of January comes from the Roman *Janus*, the God of beginnings, gates, and duality. He is depicted as having two faces, one looking back at the previous year and one forward to the new year.

I have a feeling that the typical failure of many January resolutions owes to the fact that we still have one face looking to the previous year, which is only natural. But it means the energy isn't quite right. February might actually be the clean slate we need to change for real.

So, again, what would you like to change this new year?

[YOUR JOURNAL]

OFF THE HAMSTER WHEEL

The global pandemic caused a major disruption to behaviour and habits worldwide. How we work, how we move, how we eat—all were changed, and for many of us, forever.

The World Health Organisation reported on the good and bad of these changes—including a higher incidence of walking and higher rates of alcohol consumption. Some people got back to basics baking their own bread (which became a running joke) and others couldn't resist the snacking temptation with a home office adjacent to the kitchen.

On leaving the hamster wheel of our previous office lives, we may have thought it was but a short-term displacement. Now we know the reality, and, with time, the more entrenched our post-pandemic habits and behaviours become.

For the good and the bad, what have you changed since the onset of the pandemic?

PERFECTION IS
THE ENEMY OF THE GOOD

n March 2020, as the pandemic was raging worldwide and gov-
ernments were slow to take the hard decisions, World Health
Organisation epidemiologist Dr. Michael Ryan made an impas-
sioned plea at a press conference on the dangers of delay. With
his recent experience of dealing with the ravages of the Ebola epi-
demic, he knew very well the hazards of hesitation.

His comments are gold dust for any innovation or behavioural
science professor, and I've since used them many times in my sessions. One section in particular stands out: "…everyone is afraid
of the consequence of error, but the greatest error is not to move.
Perfection is the enemy of the good."

In other words, don't be afraid of failure. How can this be
practiced?

- Learn by doing.
- Embrace experimentation.
- Have a bias towards action.

What can you do today that will keep these top-of-mind?

THE POWER OF THE MIX

O ne of my most rewarding experiences during early 2021 was teaching my Executive MBA class at IE Business School in Madrid. It was my first face-to-face work of any kind in exactly one year, which made it memorable on its own. And the experience itself was also special. Half of the class was physically in Madrid and the other half connected virtually.

Talk of hybrid is all around. Whether combining online and face-to-face learning or working from home and office-time, we are expecting a future in which we look to leverage the power of the mix.

But we shouldn't stop there in how we think about hybrid. There's another important aspect of the mix: The way you did things before and the way you did things during the pandemic.

So, moving forward, how can you combine your habits from the pre-pandemic world with your habits of the post-pandemic world? What is your own power of the mix?

EMBRACE CONSTRAINTS

I went downstairs, feeling just a little less guilty than the day before. Opening and then locking the gate behind me, I snatched another glance around to check for police. No one. Good. I then ran for 20 minutes. Each loop lasted no more than one minute so about 20 loops was the norm, around 5.5km. The boredom and dizziness had decreased in the past few days but I still felt like a hamster on a wheel.

This was my daily exercise regime at the start of lockdown in March 2020 at home in Barcelona. For six long weeks, citizens were not allowed to leave the house save for essential food shopping once a week or medical provisions. No outdoor exercise was permitted. As a lifelong athlete, exercise has always played a huge role in my overall health and wellbeing, and the lockdowns faced me with a dilemma. So, I decided to use the community space that many apartment buildings in Spain have as my private prison yard.

The result, incredibly, was that I became fitter than at any point in the past seven years. I have international experience and have trained with Olympic track athletes and Tour de France cyclists and there had been no limit to where or for how long I exercised. Yet, ironically, it was during the pandemic—when presented with huge constraints that forced me to get creative— that I saw the bigger impact.

You may face limitations in your life right now, and think it's not the time to change your behaviour. But it's the perfect time. Embrace constraints. As a start, write some of them down.

PRACTICING CHANGE

F old your arms for me please.

Now look down and see which arm is on top of the other.

Now fold your arms the other way, with the other one on top.

How does that feel?

Weird, right? Strange.

Now go back to the normal way. Aah, much better.

And again, change to the strange way. Still strange, yes, but I would contend slightly less so.

A third and fourth time and slightly less strange each time. Change, any change, gets easier with practice. One of the reasons we don't like change is that it is difficult precisely because we don't practice it enough.

Change something today. Anything. Even the way you fold your arms.

WHY HABITS EXIST

> "All our life, so far as it has definite form, is but a mass of habits—practical, emotional, and intellectual—systematically organised for our weal or woe, and bearing us irresistibly toward our destiny, whatever the latter may be."
>
> *William James*

I f it wasn't for habits, we wouldn't get very much done each day. Habits save energy. And they save us time. The shortcuts they provide allow our brains to use its limited power to do other things, and that gives us more space in our busy calendars.

Here's the thing, though: when we act via a habit, our brain stops participating fully in the decision-making process. And, for the most part, the brain doesn't distinguish between good and bad habits.

In this way, we allow habits to control us. That's the price we pay. We give away our power.

Are there any habits that you're better off without? Time to take back some power this month.

WHO KNEW?

We touch our faces more than 200 times a day.

Actually, for most of us it's probably a lot more. This is based on research of surgical residents who should know better about the risks of face touching in a hospital environment. In the early days of the pandemic in particular we were warned of the dangers of touching our face in regards to catching the virus.

What other, mostly automatic and *invisible* things might you do every day that are worthwhile paying attention to today?

MAKE IT EASY ON YOURSELF

'm a big fan of the Japanese fiction novelist Haruki Murakami. Not only do I love his stories but I'm fascinated by his writing process. A long-time triathlete and marathon runner, Murakami has commented at length on how exercise fuels his creativity, principally in the book *What I Talk About When I Talk About Running*.

I've also learned from his process for my own, modest, book-writing exploits, principally on the value of consistency. In one of his interviews, he talks of the importance of both physical and mental strength, and the value of *routine*:

> "Every day I go to my study and sit at my desk
> and put the computer on. At that moment,
> I have to open the door. It's a big, heavy door.
> It's just routine. It's kind of boring. It's a
> routine. But the routine is so important."

The metaphor of that 'heavy door' can be applied to many aspects of our lives. But, if we build a consistent routine, it makes it easy.

What can you begin to automate today? As long as you think clearly on intent, you're not giving away your power—you're strapping in for the ride.

BEHAVIOURAL AGILITY

1, 2, 3, 4, 5······
I'm in the next room, and a large smile spreads across my face.
13, 16, 14... and my smile turns into a chuckle.

It's the first months of the pandemic and my young son is practicing his counting. He speaks three languages each day and most of his school instruction is in Catalan, so we thought it a good idea to reinforce the basics at home, such as counting while he washes his hands. As he counted through the tricky teens to 20, he revealed (unbeknownst to him of course, as children often do) another element of our ingrained habits.

We have all washed our hands every day for years of course, and probably haven't thought much about it. In fact, rigorous hand-washing has been a part of public health campaigns for over 100 years. From the CDC in the US to the NHS in the UK, it remains a periodic focus for health officials who know how important it is in curbing the spread of disease.

The pandemic has made this previously invisible action highly visible. Like my son, we were told to count to 20.

As we move further into an ever-changing world what other automatic behaviours might need to be made visible? How can we use this awareness to understand and improve our own learning and agility?

MINDFUL STEPS
(PART I)

J ust because we do something every day doesn't mean we are aware of what's going on. Let me give you an example. I'm going to ask you three questions on walking, but first please, go for a short walk. Seriously. Even if it's a dozen or so steps around your home. Now, try and answer the following questions. (Answers are at the bottom of the next page).

1. Which part of the foot touches the ground first?
2. When the right foot is flat, what is the left foot doing?
3. When the left heel touches the ground, where is the right arm?

How did you do? They're not that easy, these questions. Even if you get them right, the answers don't come quickly for most people. Yet, we walk every day.

If you were to ask the same questions to a competitive race walker, or someone undergoing rehabilitation to walk again after an accident, the answers would likely be more forthcoming.

This is the difference between something that is conscious and intentional and visible and something that is subconscious, automatic, and hidden.

This is the game we play when building new habits or breaking existing ones.

INTENTION BEFORE INTENTIONALITY

S o, what do *you* want to change?

Maybe this decision is a result of your experience so far of the post-pandemic world.

What new positive habits would you like to adopt?

What existing negative habit would you like to stop?

Write down some intentions below:

the much lesser probability.) 3) In front of the body.

1) Heel. 2) Toes are touching (although it is possible that the foot is in the air, this is

* Answers for February 11th:

BABY STEPS

I f there's one thing I see derailing successful behaviour change more often than most, it's ambition. For the informed, creative class, the desire and willingness to improve ourselves and our world is a wonderful thing. Yet, reigning in that ambition is often the best way to get started with personal behaviour change, and those changes can help make a bigger societal impact down the road.

There is a huge amount of misinformation or urban myths about the amount of time it takes a habit to form. One of the more reliable sources is the well-cited research by Phillippa Lally and her team which concluded that the time taken for a habit to form depends on how complex the thing is. Simply put, the simpler something is, the quicker it is in achieving automaticity.

This is the game we talked about earlier. When moving from intentional effort to automatic habit, new synapses are being formed in the brain. When this process is complete, a new habit is formed—you have crossed the finish line after all your hard work.

But what if you are aiming for something big and ambitious? The finish line of that synaptic process is farther away. Maybe you get there. Maybe not. Life is complex. Stuff gets in the way. This is normal and shouldn't deter you from making an attempt.

Get started with baby steps. Build on success.

MARGINAL GAINS

Great Britain's track cycling team was traditionally a mediocre performer at the Olympic Games, winning just one gold medal in 100 years. Then a change occurred and they have dominated the last four Olympics (including the delayed Tokyo 2020), winning 29 golds.

Their strategy, *the cumulative effect of marginal gains*, acknowledges the tiny margins that separate winning from losing in an explosive high-speed sport. The team puts an obsessive focus on any conceivable advantage, no matter how small, in the belief that doing all these tiny things will combine to make the difference.

What potential is waiting for you in the margins? And that of your team? How about your family?

The accumulation will come from daily practice. Look for something that is, or could be, part of your everyday. Make it better.

What you do everyday matters more, much more, than what you do every now and then.

FEBRUARY 15TH

EXPONENTIAL GAIN

1% better every day for a year: 1.01 x 365 = 37.78%
1% worse every day for a year: 0.99 x 365 = 0.03%
This is the compound interest of a small yet consistent effort.

DEVIL IN THE DETAILS

Having studied and then consulted in the field of design, I've long been fascinated in breakthrough insights and where they come from. The surprising thing is that these *a-ha* moments often come from the most mundane parts of our life. The key is looking at the details and accepting the fact opportunity can reveal itself at any time Monday through Sunday, whether that is in the first ten minutes of our day, during the morning commute, while you run errands, or when you walk through your front door coming home from work. All areas of daily life are rich and teeming with possibility for change.

If you want to be successful with tweaking your behaviour, be specific. Give it details. Every single step.

- What time of day will your new habit take place?
- How long will it last?
- Where are you?
- What usually happens before?
- What usually happens afterwards?
- Who else is involved?
- What objects or tools are used?

USE THE TRIGGER

We live in a world of constant triggers. The Big Tech revolution created a war for attention that seldom leaves us in peace. Pings, dings, rings, red bubble notifications, and more vie for our limited attention and energy. Even a specific time of day, place, or other person can trigger certain responses.

We can also use the trigger to our advantage.

What already exists in your daily life? Perhaps it is something that you have done for many years—a rock-solid routine such as the morning shower, brushing your teeth, or preparing a meal. We all have many instances of things that make up the bedrock of our daily behaviours and actions.

Here's what you do:

Place a desired change immediately before or after something you already do on a routine basis. This gives it support. It will make the new thing memorable and stronger.

THE HABIT LOOP

I do squats in the shower.

I may look daft but it's not as if anyone sees me. It's probably the strongest new habit I've added to my routine in the past several years. Here's what I do: I wash my hair and before rinsing out the shampoo, I do 20 squats. That's at least 140 squats per week, or 7,280 squats per year, and a powerful cumulative impact from an achievable daily habit.

My trigger or *cue* is not the shower, it's the shampoo. If I don't wash my hair, I don't end up doing the squats. The cue is that specific and that's what makes it work.

Every habit has a before, a cue or signal, and an after, a reward and reason for keeping doing it.

Habit loops can be used to stop bad habits too. For example, I replaced the socialization reward from smoking with other social rituals and no longer charge my phone on my bedside table as a way to eliminate the cue of scrolling in bed. Instead of tackling a bad habit head-on, think about eliminating the cue or replacing the reward.

Don't just think about the habit or action, consider the before and after. What's the habit loop?

DON'T GO IT ALONE

Telefónica CEO José María Álvarez-Pallete López uses Twitter. Quite a bit actually. When I interviewed him about his habits just before he became CEO, he talked at length about the importance of daily reading blocks. One 30-minute period in the morning on arriving at the office, and another in the evening.

Actively using Twitter may seem counterintuitive to this but I think the biggest value for him of using the platform is sharing with the world what he reads and finds valuable. If anything, his 83,000 followers hold him accountable to his daily reading habit which is an important part of his executive wellbeing.

Accountability is powerful. Involve someone else in your behaviour change—a colleague, spouse, a son or daughter—who will keep you on track. Even a pet. My beloved sheepdog Harry held me accountable with a walking after dinner commitment several years ago. Animals catch a routine very quickly. I didn't want to continue past the first few weeks but Harry would sit by the door and begin to bark as soon as I finished dinner.

Don't go it alone.

DON'T BREAK THE CHAIN

Brad Isaac was a young comedian when he met Jerry Seinfeld at a comedy club. On asking Seinfeld if he had any tips for a young comic, he shared the following, which Isaac recounted in an interview with Lifehacker:

> He said the way to be a better comic was to create better jokes and the way to create better jokes was to write every day.
>
> He told me to get a big wall calendar that has a whole year on one page and hang it on a prominent wall. The next step was to get a big red magic marker. He said for each day that I do my task of writing, I get to put a big red X over that day.
>
> "After a few days you'll have a chain. Just keep at it and the chain will grow longer every day. You'll like seeing that chain, especially when you get a few weeks under your belt. Your only job is to not break the chain."

I recently had the pleasure of hearing from someone whose life had changed after following my advice to build a streak in order to ingrain habits. He had recently hit a 1,000-day streak on Duolingo, and now has a competent grasp of Japanese. All those snatched moments add up in a similar fashion to the British Cycling strategy.

This in turn inspired me and my family has since started using Duolingo at home to learn Italian. *Grazie* Riaz! (and Jerry).

38,000 PUSH-UPS (SO FAR...)

O n the 1st of May 2019, I did 20 push-ups and WhatsApp'd my brother who did the same. The next day he did 22 and messaged me. We went on like this, adding two each day, till we had reached 80 at the end of the month. June 1st arrived and so did a well-deserved rest back to 20. And this is how the concept of 'ping-pong-push-ups' was born.

As I write this entry, my most recent set was 46 and am averaging 18,000 push-ups per year. Without the streak, I'd be lucky to do a few hundred. It's still hard most days but the streak makes it easy to keep going. It's the push I need. That's the thing about behaviour change and impact of good ritual design. A habit can be hard and easy at the same time.

I'm a long way off from Ron Hill's literal running streak of 52 years and 39 days. To that point, I'm not sure streaks are wholly positive when obsession is in the mix as was the case with some of Hill's exploits, but for now, it's working for me. What kind of streak can you begin today?

WE LIVE IN
A PHYSICAL WORLD

I n an ever-increasing virtual life, it's easy to forget the importance of our physical environment and how it shapes behaviour. Perhaps you were inspired to take the stairs on a more regular basis after reading January's nudges. How have you encountered any of the natural barriers of conventional building design that we commented on January 13th?

We can actively shape our surroundings to create visual cues or nudges to support positive behaviour and inhibit the negative. For my morning mat Pilates routine, which I have followed for several years now, I have benefitted from my mat being in plain view and near the kitchen and water machine that I habitually walk to each morning upon waking. My wife may prefer I choose a more discreet location for the mat but I know I need it there to nudge me towards action.

Look around you today. How can you re-design your physical surroundings to better support your habit intentions?

HOW TO EAT
LESS CHOCOLATE

And you tell me, no, no. I'm very happy with my level of chocolate consumption thank you very much.

But if you do want to lower it, what do you do? Don't buy it!

Want to sit less in the office, or at home? Remove the chair. Drill down to the basics on your surroundings.

GET NEW FRIENDS

"You are the average of the five people you
spend the most time with."

Jim Rohn

Our physical environment is a key determinant of our behaviour—and that includes our social environment. We may think the things we do and say each day are a result of our own conscious choice (which eventually becomes our subconscious habits) yet they are also a reflection of the things other people say and do, especially those with whom we spend a lot of time. We imitate and are imitated. The pandemic emphasised the social aspect of our human nature. Whether it was a sudden burst of online quizzes and virtual coffees, or simply missing the human contact and buzz of the office, many of us understood our need for connection.

In *Harvard Business Review,* Jason Corsello and Dylan Minor reported on the 'positive knowledge spill-overs' of physically moving an underperforming employee to sit next to a star employee as a way to quietly yet effectively address performance issues.

During training programs, I try to highlight, in a humorous fashion, the critical impact that our social interactions have on our own behaviour: What do you do if you want to stop smoking and all your friends smoke?

Get new friends.

THE 7 HACKS OF HIGHLY EFFECTIVE HABITS

The past week or so of nudges have been based on a model I've delivered for more than a decade. *The 7 Hacks of Highly Effective Habits* is not a scientific model. Though it is based on some research, both mine and others, it is derived mostly from experience. The seven hacks are 'sticky'—useful and memorable in mobilising people to change. They are:

- Small
- Specific
- Supported
- Shared
- Streak
- Surroundings
- Social

The title is a play on words inspired by Stephen Covey's *Seven Habits of Highly Effective People*. Though it is an important work, it has resulted in a constant stream of clickbait articles that advise readers on which habits to adopt and to stop. With advice coming in from all angles, the process can seem overwhelming at times.

Decide for yourself. Experiment with the hacks above, using whatever combination fits into your changing life context.

ME AND MY
COFFEE GRINDER

I have a manual coffee grinder. I get up early and grind coffee. I'm never yet fully awake and grinding coffee by hand is hard work. I could pop in a coffee capsule and make my life easier, but I love the details of this morning ritual. There is a special moment when I begin to smell the freshly ground coffee and hear it slipping out of the stainless-steel grinder as I empty it into the coffee filter.

Rituals are more than habits or behaviours. They are imbued with meaning and purpose. They satisfy deep-lying needs. We may talk of rituals within the context of religion or history, but might not readily associate them with our own life and work, our day-to-day.

Don't forget, though, that our pre-pandemic world of work was full of ritual. There was that early morning commute or the afternoon watercooler catch-up. Maybe you had a regular Friday celebration with the team afterwork or a scheduled lunch with peers. All served a purpose. All disappeared, at least temporarily. Perhaps we have since found that we miss some of these rituals and not others. Maybe there are some that we didn't expect to miss, like how the trip to and from the office served as an important transition ritual between home and work and gave us the best chance of being present in both places.

- What rituals are important for you?
- What purpose do they serve?
- Which artefacts or objects are important for these rituals?

FUNCTIONAL AND EMOTIONAL NEEDS

I n many cases we found it easy to replace elements of our pre-pandemic lives on a functional level, but what were you (or still are today) missing on a more emotional level from that time?

For example, it might only now that you realise that during business trips, flying gave you a special 30-second meditation before the plane sped down the runway, or that the overnight stay gave you a chance to invest in your own self, momentarily away from family and professional duties.

Be pro-active in designing for your emotional needs.

Ask yourself what you're missing from your previous working life and start to actively design rituals in different spaces, considering both time and place. Perhaps you will come up with a new weekend ritual, or a way to mark the day's start or finish. And don't forget the non-work elements if you're spending more time working from home which may include mealtimes or connecting deeply with family.

Re-design your rituals and routines (a new version of R&R). Cater to your emotional needs. Create the boundaries necessary so that work and life don't create a messy middle.

FIND YOUR KEYSTONE

"A keystone habit is a pattern which has the power to start a chain-reaction, changing other habits as it moves through your life."

Charles Duhigg

I get up early. Usually around 6:30 and preferably pre-dawn. I do this even if I get to bed late the night before. If I don't do it, I don't feel like myself.

This is my keystone habit. It's the thing that makes everything else fall into place. I start my day early and in a quiet, calm fashion and I either walk the dog or go for a run before the city chaos begins. It also means that, because I'm tired sooner that day, I get to bed early too. Thanks to the fact that I'm calm and exercise, I make better eating choices too.

What's the one thing you need that makes everything else fall into place? Over the years, I've talked to people who have identified big areas like sleep, exercise, meditation, and eating, and more specific things like a family dinner or making the bed.

Have you found your keystone habit this month? If so, write it below.

If not, keep searching.

DO SOMETHING SPECIAL

t doesn't happen every year. Do something special.
Maybe this becomes your February 29th habit.

NOTES ON YOUR JOURNEY THROUGH HABITS IN FEBRUARY:

MARCH

SLEEP

ARE YOU INTERESTED?

From Matthew Walker's *Why We Sleep*:

> "Scientists have discovered a revolutionary
> new treatment that makes you live longer.
> It enhances your memory, makes you more
> attractive. It keeps you slim and lowers food
> cravings. It protects you from cancer and
> dementia. It wards off colds and flu. It lowers
> your risk of heart attacks and stroke, not to
> mention diabetes. You'll even feel happier,
> less depressed, and less anxious. Are you
> interested?"

If it was a pill, we would buy them by the bucket-load. Getting more
(and better) sleep is a trickier proposition. Let's see what we can do
about that this month.

ARE YOU GETTING ENOUGH?

t's very often the first question, so here's the answer:
Around 90% of the population need between seven and eight hours of sleep each night.

It's a bell-curve distribution so that means there will be people on the lower end of the curve who need less and others who need more. Yet these outlier groups are, by far, in the minority.

I often ask people how much sleep they get and what I typically find is that the largest segment is six to seven hours. It's possible that's all they need but, following the logic above, the probability is that they are just *slightly* sleep deprived.

Maybe this applies to you. Try to add 30 more minutes of sleep starting tonight. See what happens.

BECOMING A WORLD-CLASS SLEEPER

As a young athlete I was conscious of trying to get a few nights of good sleep before an important race. I thought of this again when reading an interview with Roger Federer who said he sleeps around ten hours each night during an important tournament.

Spanish football club Real Madrid have 81 bedrooms at their training complex for players and staff to sleep or nap, each tailored specifically for the individual. In the English league a few seasons ago, Southampton took it to another level in an effort to improve their results away from home. They booked the team hotel for two nights instead of one. Club staff arrived on the first night to deep clean the already clean rooms and place bespoke mattresses tailored to each player. The duvets, pillow cases and sheets were then washed and ironed by the club, using the same washing powder and the same methods. Wherever the players travelled with the team, their bed would smell and feel the same.

Sleep is something we do every day, so it's not for lack of practice that we're not all excellent sleepers. In many ways, we just need to approach our sleep in a more intentional way. What is high performance in sleep? Ask yourself the following questions to get started:

- How refreshed/rested do you feel waking in the morning?
- How many times do you remember waking up during the night?
- How fast do you fall asleep after getting into bed?

Many elite athletes have the luxury of sleep coaches, but you can become your own. Use the nudges this month to become a world-class sleeper.

CHANGE THE WORLD

I t's not just physical or sporting gains that we get from sleep, our cognitive performance is improved too.

In "Change the World and Get to Bed by 10pm" *Harvard Business Review* reported on research from *Nature* journal which found sleep deprivation, specifically hours of wakefulness, to have the same negative impact on cognitive performance as alcohol intake. So, working late into the night and missing out on sleep might not be the best idea.

Research shows that, while routine thinking can proceed unhindered by sleep deprivation, the higher order thinking—creativity, planning, judgement—called 'executive function', can be severely affected.

You may not put it on your CV anytime soon but sleep is a key professional skill.

LEADING BY EXAMPLE

I n executive leadership circles, the traditional view of sleep is that it's a waste of time. There have been countless examples over the years of 'high-flyers' who boast of getting by on four hours sleep a night, and who urge the rest of us to follow their lead.

This will change.

McKinsey reported on the dimensions of high-performance leadership that are supported by better sleep. An orientation towards results, solving problems, seeking different perspectives, and supporting others were all shown to be made better by the attention, concentration, memory, and other mental capacities that are known to improve with sleep.

Foster School of Business management professor Chris Barnes focuses on the effects of sleep on management and leadership. Some of his findings are quite fascinating, and show the deep impact of even subtle differences related to sleep. For example, he has found that when leaders deliver a speech and are perceived to be sleep deprived by their audience, their message comes across as less inspiring, regardless of the content.

A good day at work starts the night before. Get a good night's sleep. Lead by example.

RIDING THE ROLLERCOASTER

Sleep is a mystery.

For something we spend years of our life doing, not to mention a field of study that has been deeply researched by leading scientists for decades, this may come as a surprise. New findings are emerging all the time, but it still remains a mystery. Yet we do know the basics.

One of the first areas of understanding in regards to what happens when we sleep is *sleep cycles*.

When we fall asleep, we move progressively into and out of a deeper state of sleep. Stage one, stage two, stage three, stage four. Then we come back up: three, two, one, to complete a full cycle. Each cycle, or *ultradian rhythm* lasts around 90 minutes.

Effectively, we ride a rollercoaster each night. And most of us ride it five times. The key is to make those rides as clean and deep as possible.

The rest of this month is geared simply towards enjoying the ride.

7 DAYS A WEEK

Cycles are a huge part of who we are.

The good news is that transformation of our sleeping ability, and more generally health and wellbeing, can be facilitated by simply respecting our natural cycles.

The first item to consider is our sleep-wake cycle:

- What time do you normally go to bed?
- What time do you normally wake up?

If you are like most people, you will have the same answers for Monday to Friday (or Sunday to Thursday depending on where you live) and another for the weekend. Yet our sleep-wake cycle runs seven days a week. Our brain craves consistency.

We shouldn't punish ourselves of course and if non-working days can benefit from a little extra sleep or a later night, then great. But if you have a significant difference between your workday and weekend sleep-wake cycle you will suffer a series of negative impacts which begin with the quality and quantity of your sleep.

Go for better alignment. Seven days a week.

SLEEP DEBT

How much do you owe?

One of the main reasons many of us have for sleeping more on the weekend is to pay back the sleep debt accrued during the working week. Let's face it, some young parents and many executives have been sleep-deprived for most of their adult lives and don't know the difference. Over time, though, erratic behaviour or a lack of patience may be assumed as natural parts of a personality.

In addition to behavioural changes, research shows other ways continual sleep debt can impact us. In a remarkable sleep deprivation study from 2003 led by Hans Van Dongen from the University of Pennsylvania School of Medicine, subjects who got six hours of sleep a night for two weeks straight functioned as poorly as those who were forced to stay awake for two days in a row.

The good news is that there's no Rip Van Winkle scenario (who fell asleep for 20 years in the short story by Washington Irving) and you can actually pay back sleep debt—even years of it—in just a matter of days. Here's what you do:

Pick a week where you don't need to be up at a required time (for example during vacation).

- Go to bed when you feel sleepy.
- Don't set an alarm.
- Wake up naturally.

That's it. You'll probably find that you sleep long the first few days, paying back sleep debt before settling into a pattern—and this pattern will be your own natural sleep-wake cycle.

LIGHT AND DARK CYCLES

W e've evolved over thousands of years being awake during the day when the sun was shining, and asleep at night when the sun has set. Like most animals, we are *diurnal*.

But modern society is increasingly displacing these natural light and dark cycles. Two things happen:

- We don't get enough natural daylight during the day. Studies show we spend up to 90% of our lives inside a building. Though new forms of 'circadian' lighting do help, most artificial light doesn't have the same benefits (or anywhere near the LUX, or light intensity factor) of natural light.
- We get too much artificial light at night—mobile devices, laptops, TVs, home lighting, light pollution in cities—it's all around us.

The key factor is that we have a gland between our eyes, the pineal gland, which emits melatonin, the sleep hormone. The normal biological process involves melatonin production through the pineal gland as the light fades at the end of a day. If you shine bright light into that gland, say, from your mobile device at night, melatonin production is suppressed.

Scientists call this continual displacement of our light and dark cycles *social jet lag*.

The simple takeaway: get more natural daylight during the day and be careful with light at night.

BEWARE THE NIGHT SHIFT

B ecause we are diurnal, not nocturnal, sleeping during the day and staying awake at night isn't natural.

Studies show that long-term night shift workers have a range of health problems including obesity, cardiovascular disease, chronic fatigue, and depression.

If you're expected to work the nightshift, I'm sorry but there's no better news for you. At least try and make the situation a temporary reality and keep in mind that when changing shift patterns, you will need a few days adjustment.

Try not to reduce sleep duration, get enough daylight exposure (to ensure sufficient levels of Vitamin D among other benefits) and be careful with food choices, because the body tends to crave more starch based, instant energy sources at night.

Things to keep in mind even if you don't work the night shift.

YOUR OWN CYCLE

re you a Lark, an Owl, or neither?

1. *How's your appetite in the first half hour after you wake up?*
   (a) Very poor [1] (b) Fairly poor [2]
   (c) Fairly good [3] (d) Very good [4]

2. *For the first half hour after you wake up in the morning, how do you feel?*
   (a) Very sleepy [1] (b) Fairly sleepy [2]
   (c) Fairly alert [3] (d) Very alert [4]

3. *You have no commitments the next day; at what time would you go to bed compared with your usual bedtime?*
   (a) Seldom or never later [4]
   (b) Less than one hour later [3]
   (c) 1–2 hours later [2] (d) More than 2 hours later [1]

4. *You are going to get fit. A friend suggests joining their fitness class between 7am and 8am. How do you think you'd perform?*
   (a) Would be on good form [4]
   (b) Would be on reasonable form [3]
   (c) Would find it difficult [2]
   (d) Would find it very difficult [1]

5. *At what time do you feel sleepy and in need to go to bed?*
   (a) 8–9pm [5] (b) 9–10:15pm [4] (c) 10:15pm–12:45am [3]
   (d) 12:45–2am [2] (e) 2–3am [1]

continued to next page

continued from previous page

6. *If you went to bed at 11pm, how sleepy would you be?*
   (a) Not at all sleepy [0] (b) A little sleepy [2]
   (c) Fairly sleepy [3] (d) Very sleepy [5]

7. *One night you have to remain awake between 4 and 6am.*
   You have no commitments the next day.
   Which suits you best?
   (a) Not go to bed until 6am [1]
   (b) Nap before 4am and nap after 6am [2]
   (c) Sleep before 4am and nap after 6am [3]
   (d) Sleep before 4am and remain awake after 6am [4]

8. *Suppose that you can choose your own work hours, but*
   have to work five hours during the day. When would you
   like to start work?
   (a) Midnight–5am [1] (b) 3–8am [5] (c) 8–10am [4]
   (d) 10am–2pm [3] (e) 2–4pm [2] (f) 4pm–midnight [1]

9. *At what time of day do you feel your best?*
   (a) Midnight–5am [1] (b) 5am–9am [5]
   (c) 9am–11am [4] (d) 11am–5pm [3]
   (e) 5pm–10pm [2] (f) 10pm–midnight [1]

10. *Do you think of yourself as a morning or evening person?*
    (a) Morning type [6] (b) More morning than evening [4]
    (c) More evening than morning [2] (d) Evening type [0]

Scoring
8–12: Strong Owl; 13–20: Moderate Owl; 21–33: neither Owl nor
Lark; 34–41: Moderate Lark; 42–46: Strong Lark

LARKS V OWLS

The Lark or Owl quiz can be found on March 11th.

It's a battle for the ages. Like cyclists v runners. Or vampires v werewolves. Ok not quite, but still, what does some of the research say about these two types of people, the larks v the owls?

First of all, I know it can be a tad underwhelming if you find yourself in the middle, neither one or the other. We tend to like the definitive identity that labels like this can give. In some ways, however, it is good news because if you find yourself not quite a lark and not quite an owl, this is the most balanced outcome and it allows you to flex more easily to one side or the other.

Society tends to favour Larks, with most current structures around the workplace celebrating the work ethic of the 'early riser'. And this attitude also affects Larks themselves who can be judgemental of Owls and consider them to be lazy, when on the contrary they often just have a more laid-back attitude.

Societal conditioning, including work and family commitments, will create more of a Lark profile as we age. This is true even for those who had a strong Owl preference as teenagers, a period in our lives when our sleep patterns undergo a substantial shift.

In my work with organisations over the years, I've found managers are more often Larks and creatives more often Owls. I once gave a workshop to 60 CEOs. 59 were Larks. The solitary Owl was delighted and said to me: *"I used to have my main meeting at 8am because I thought that's simply what CEOs do. Now I understand it's what Larks do. I'm now going to have the meeting when I'm more alert."*

Now that you have a better idea of your own Lark v Owl tendencies, can you guess those of the people around you?

BECOMING OWLISH

The Lark or Owl quiz can be found on March 11th.

C hanging from being a strong Lark to a strong Owl or vice-versa, at least in a short time-frame (we're talking less than a decade or two), isn't biologically feasible. Committing to an early morning routine as part of the vaunted '5am club' should therefore be treated with care.

Yet, we can nudge ourselves one way or the other depending on our needs.

Maybe you're a Lark and you want to be more Owl? Say, for example, you have a 10pm business dinner in Madrid—but you're normally in bed at that time!

Try playing with natural daylight. Stay indoors during the first half of the day and gain as much outdoor light exposure in the afternoon to improve alertness toward the second half of the day.

BECOMING LARKISH

The Lark or Owl quiz can be found on March 11th.

M aybe you're an Owl and you want to be more Lark? What if you have an important meeting or presentation at 8am but ideally, you'd still be sleeping.

Set your alarm for pre-dawn. Once you grudgingly do get up, go outside in order to get the maximum amount of daylight exposure as soon as the sun rises, perhaps with a gentle walk or some meditation.

This won't be easy and harder still to make it sustainable due to the simple fact that Owls find it difficult to get themselves to bed early. Gaining the maximum amount of sunlight (going outside, even on a cloudy day, still makes a significant difference) during the first half of the day will help to ensure your natural 'clock' begins to wind down a little sooner each day.

A 24-HOUR SOCIETY?

Though society has traditionally given morning-types an easier ride, I do believe the Fourth Industrial Revolution, accelerated by the flexibility and hybrid nature of a post-pandemic world, will better cater to the needs of all. This means that knowing your chronotype preference and respecting that of others will be more important.

Think about your home environment. Is it difficult to have an important conversation with your partner early in the morning or late at night? Your chronotypes may be vastly different. At work, when does your team have their best ideas? Highest energy? A Lark working a late schedule or an Owl working an early schedule is a chronotype mismatch that can be problematic. Leaders should understand that employees are not being lazy or disinterested in the work, simply that their biology doesn't support their working patterns.

The danger is that this leads to a non-stop society (some may argue we're already there) and there is a fine balance to be struck between catering to different needs and infringing on the needs of all.

If you keep sleep and rest as a top priority in your own life today, and every day, you'll have the best chance of striking that balance.

THE WAY WE SLEEP AROUND HERE (PART I)

C ulture may be commonly defined as *the way we do things around here.* Often applied to the world of work, the sum of people's habits also defines a specific culture in all aspects of our lives. To that point, the approach to sleep can vary markedly from one country to the next.

On moving from Scotland to the Basque Country in 2003, part of my initial culture shock was related to sleep. Perhaps my first noisy night sleeping (or trying to) in the middle of Bilbao old town on the weekend was a sign of things to come.

Everything in Spain just seemed to be *later.* I'm still amazed to this day at the time babies and infants stay up to, compared to the UK. And, even though I have been going on work visits to the Middle East for several years, I'm still amazed at how *early* everything is.

People often need help adjusting. The footballer Gareth Bale is a good example—he made a big money move from Tottenham to Real Madrid and had some initial performance issues that were eventually addressed by employing the services of a sleep coach. The way people live their lives, including the typical sleep-wake cycle, varies significantly between London and Madrid.

Our basic sleep needs are mostly universal, but how they are satisfied is often very different.

THE WAY WE SLEEP AROUND HERE (PART II)

As an increasing amount of people can *work from anywhere* and are thus now interested in finding the most attractive destinations worldwide to do that, perhaps it is relevant to take a more detailed look at global sleep attitudes.

Sleep duration varies significantly around the world. The proliferation of sleep tracking devices in recent years has allowed for a variety of research and one major app, *Sleep Cycle*, has reported that New Zealand, Finland, and the Netherlands get the most sleep with more than seven and a half hours. South Korea, Saudi Arabia, and Japan get the least amount of sleep at less than six and a half hours.

It's no wonder then that napping in public places, or *inemuri*—sleeping while present, is common in Japan. Dozing is sometimes done on a park bench or a commuter train, at a dinner party or even during a meeting at work. In a culture that values diligence, napping in public is taken as a sign that a person is tired from working hard but still wants to participate in the current moment.

In Scandinavian countries such as Norway and Sweden, parents often leave their babies outdoors to nap in their strollers, even in the middle of winter. Parents believe the fresh air is good for their kids and that being outside will help keep young children from getting sick. Many day care centers and pre-schools hold naptime outside to give babies this exposure.

Wherever you are, think about creating your own culture at home.

SLEEP HYGIENE

What we do when awake affects how we sleep. How we move, how we eat, what we do in the time leading up to sleep—all have an impact.

Good habits for sleep come under the area of sleep hygiene, such as how you prepare for sleep and the things you do, eat and drink in the hours leading up to bedtime. Consider your own sleep hygiene now before we dig into the details in the coming days. Perhaps even note down what you do each day, and how you feel when you wake up the next morning.

I THINK SOME OF MY GOOD SLEEP HABITS ARE:

I THINK SOME OF MY BAD SLEEP HABITS ARE:

WHERE THE MAGIC HAPPENS

When was the last time you considered making your bedroom as fit as possible for the purpose of sleeping? Here's an initial checklist to get started:

Sound
Is the bedroom the quietest room in your home? How can you make it quieter?

Light
Can you make the bedroom as dark as required? Some people don't like pitch darkness but neither do we want to be woken up at 5am mid-summer thanks to the light curtains covering the window.

Temperature
We sleep best in a cool environment, with studies showing 16–18°C as the ideal range.

Digital
Take the TV out. Watch out for other blinking lights and LEDs that might disturb you in the middle of the night. Charge your phone in another room. Find an alternative alarm clock.

Bed
When was the last time you bought a new mattress? Do some research on your required firmness. Treat yourself to expensive sheets that mean going to bed each night is a relaxing pleasure.

WOULD YOU LIKE TO SEE THE MENU MADAM?

Perhaps it's just a result of my ageing but I often find one of the trickiest things about business travel to be the hotel pillows. Mattresses and sheets seem to be a more or less standard quality but, even in the better hotels, pillows are a trickier prospect. The impact of a sprained neck might ruin the following day or, as has been the case with some travelling athletes, the loss of a competition (and the prize money that might come along with it). Many athletes and frequent travellers pack their own pillow.

And many hotels now provide a pillow menu for guests to get the best night's rest possible. Of course, after a long day, a detailed pillow menu might be the last thing you want to review. But it can make a difference. So, keep it simple. Look out for firmness (soft, medium, firm) and breathability/temperature retention among the complexity.

SLEEP POSITIONS

My wife slept sitting up for the last three months of her pregnancy. Acid reflux, a common issue for women in their last trimester, was unbearable for her. What's your preferred sleeping position?

- The *fetal position* is beneficial for lower back pain and can reduce snoring, though it may limit deep breathing and can result in stiffness. Placing a pillow between your knees can help.
- *Sleeping on your side*, particularly on the left can reduce heartburn and aid digestion, though it can result in shoulder and jaw stiffness.
- *Sleeping on your stomach* might be the worst option, though it does reduce snoring, because it can cause significant neck and back pain as well as pressure on different muscles and joints meaning you wake up feeling tired. If you do sleep on your stomach, try to draw one leg up by your side.
- *Flat on your back* is often considered the best option because it protects the spine and helps maintain good alignment along the length of your spine. Having the right height and firmness of both pillow and mattress is important to aid this alignment and reduce pressure.

Whichever way you fall asleep, you'll likely move around during the night. And that's a good thing—your body in this instance likes variety, rather than being in the same position for several hours at a time.

PREPARING FOR SLEEP

W e have an alarm to wake us up in the morning. What about for the opposite end of the sleep-wake cycle? Going to bed is another matter. What cues you to know it's time to go to bed? Do you follow a particular process?

The brainwaves of a relaxed state are similar to the brainwaves of stage one sleep, so think of some pre-bed ritual that gives you the best chance of falling asleep fast.

Maybe you divide this into *dos* and *don'ts*. Some ideas are noted below. What else can you add to the list?

> *Dos*:
> Meditation. Reading. A hot bath or shower an hour before bed (body temperature naturally dips towards bedtime and some studies show this additional aid helps falling asleep)…

> *Don'ts*:
> TV or mobile device in the last 60 minutes.
> Alcohol or caffeine in the last three hours…

FALLING ASLEEP

One of the biggest benefits in my own mindful approach to sleep these past few years is falling asleep fast. Normally, I go to bed and within 60 seconds, I'm asleep. If I'm really lucky I will wake up, naturally, at a consistent time each morning. I have however, experienced many nights when falling asleep—on first going to bed and again after waking in the middle of the night—has seemed an impossible task. If that sounds like you, try the following:

- Go to bed as soon as you feel tired—that first wave of tiredness is the production of melatonin, the sleep hormone. If you tough it out, you may find it harder to fall asleep later.
- During the day we breathe predominantly through our chest. At night, through the belly. To fall asleep faster, or fall asleep again after waking during the night, focus on belly breathing.
- Waking up in the middle of the night is perfectly natural because of the sleep cycle 'rollercoaster ride'. Don't over-stress in your effort to fall back asleep, which makes it harder to actually do so, called *paradoxical intention*. I know it's difficult in these situations but, do your best to relax.
- If the same thing is spinning around your head, write it down on a notepad so you can mentally put it to the side. You'll find the 3am panic is never as bad when you look at it when the sun is shining.

Like anything, it gets easier with practice, so try experimenting with your sleep tonight.

SLEEPING ON A PLANE

've been fascinated by people who are frequent long-haul travellers. When I ask them how they do it, they simply say, 'I can sleep well on a plane'.

So, how can you do it too? Let's be honest. A business class ticket and the chance of a flatbed would be a big help.

For many of us, this luxury isn't always an option, but you can adopt the logic of sleep-hygiene to your travels. Easier said than done given the amount of temptation when on the road, but bear in mind the following areas:

- Make your body tired before traveling by doing some exercise. There is a difference between being tired (good) and over-tired or sleep deprived (bad).
- Think about taking your own pillow so you have some degree of familiarity and comfort.
- And of course, take care with alcohol and over-eating. Many people complain about jetlag after a long trip of barely moving, non-stop eating and drinking, and binge-watching movies. That isn't jet lag, it's a hangover!

JET LAG

J et lag happens. Anything we do to address the often-brutal impact our bodies experience when crossing multiple time zones is about mitigating those affects. Consider the following:

- Anticipate the time change by moving toward the destination time over a period of days before your departure—even a little can help. This movement may also be done during the travel if, for example, you have a layover, or even on the plane. Since light exposure is key here, opening the window blind can help.
- Ensure that you are well rested and not sleep deprived before your trip. A large homeostatic (sleep) pressure will exacerbate jet lag effects.
- When you arrive, switch to local time immediately. Go outside and get some sunshine. This will help your natural circadian clock to reset as quickly as possible.
- If you really need to sleep during the day at your destination, either take a short 20-minute nap or a full sleep cycle (usually 90 minutes).

This has helped me on long-haul night flights when I felt nothing else could. When I arrive to my destination, I spend a few hours outside, seeing the sights or buying last minute supplies, before returning to my room, drawing the curtains for total darkness and setting my alarm for 90 minutes—one full go on the roller-coaster from stage one to four, and back again.

That's enough of a reset to make the rest of my trip a success.

WAKING UP

"Whenever you have trouble getting up in the
morning, remind yourself that you've been
made by nature for the purpose of working with
others, whereas even unthinking animals share
sleeping. And it's our own natural purpose that
is more fitting and more satisfying."

Marcus Aurelius

P erhaps the quote above is more appropriate for the theme of
purpose that we will cover in August, but it's comforting to
know that even Roman emperor philosopher-warriors found
it difficult to get up in the morning!

What is important to note here, in regards to sleep, is that
we wake according to meaning. The REM phase in particular is a
paradoxical stage of sleep that has the hallmarks of both light and
deep sleep. Scientists believe we developed REM in order to scan
our environment and keep a watchful eye on danger even when
asleep. Hence, we may continue sleeping through a loud noise
that is familiar and non-threatening but will wake when someone
whispers our name.

Two more things to consider, one a staple of sleeping advice
and the other a little more left-field:

- First off, the snooze button is not your friend! It will
  often make you feel worse for the rest of the day and
  disrupts your internal clock.
- Second, if you really struggle each morning to get up,
  practice it. Literally. During the day, practice getting
  in and out of bed to familiarise the muscle memory in
  your body.

THE NAP ZONE

N apping is not for lazy people. It is an important means of maintaining performance used by airline pilots, the world's best athletes, and astronauts.

The nap zone usually occurs around mid-afternoon, typically around 2–3pm, when our sleep pressure builds since waking and intersects with our circadian rhythm, which has a natural dip of alertness.

Numerous studies from the likes of including Harvard and NASA show napping to have an important performance benefit and this has even organisations with hard business cultures such as consultants increasingly installing rooms where people can rest and nap.

Maybe the term 'caught napping' will soon be replaced? Consider the feasibility of taking a short nap today, especially if you have a long day in prospect.

DIPPING BELOW THE SURFACE

D id you try having a nap yesterday?

There are many ways to make nap time work for you, including finding the right place and how to time it (for example a phone alarm or a dose of caffeine which takes fifteen minutes to enter the bloodstream and works as an effective wake-up). Just don't forget two things:

- The more you practice the better you will be.
  Don't try too hard, especially since time is limited.
  Bringing your resting heart rate lower and closing
  your eyes has tremendous benefit even if you don't
  actually fall asleep.

- Most important of all, limit your nap to twenty
  minutes. If you go longer, you go deeper into the
  sleep cycle. Becoming skilled at *dipping below the
  surface* of your daily sleep-wake reality, even on
  more than one occasion, can transform your life.

GOING DEEP

I f gaining competence in napping is about dipping just below the surface, then ensuring sufficient deep sleep is another important objective.

Studies show that we enjoy less deep sleep (as well as sleeping less overall) as we age and that this is a contributory factor in age-related diseases. Maximising duration and depth of sleep is important for healthy ageing.

As well as considering all the nudges this month, particularly those around sleep hygiene and preparing for sleep, remember one thing:

- Move more during the day. A highly sedentary day may result in your falling asleep but it also contributes to a fitful sleep and experiencing a shallow set of cycles during the night.

The deeper you live your day, both physically and mentally, the deeper you will reset.

CORONASOMNIA

So how did the global trauma of the pandemic affect your sleep? Was your sleep better or worse? Longer or shorter? Philips surveyed 13,000 adults in thirteen countries at the beginning of the pandemic, and found that 70% experienced one or more new sleep challenges with women more likely than men to experience difficulty. However, the survey also found that more people are now adopting strategies to improve their sleep, including meditation, reading, soothing music, and technology aids. It could be that 'Coronasomnia' provided the necessary nudge for people to be more intentional about sleep, so that their longer-term practice is now better.

What about you? Think back of what your sleep was like during the pandemic and how it has been more recently during this month of nudges. What are some of the intentions you can commit to going forward?

THE GREAT SLEEP RESET

Numerous studies show that when we sleep the brain undergoes a type of *cleaning*, removing the toxins that have built up during a busy day. It's our chance to reset and get ready to go again the next day.

Your daily reset, the precious opportunity we all have to start again each day, begins the night before.

APRIL

ENERGY

A PRECIOUS RESOURCE

[MY JOURNAL]

Does energy wane as we age? I've certainly had my own reflections on this and sense of alarm that my life-force was draining away! When I became a parent at 38 years-old I was acutely aware of the change in my own energy. I've since settled on a more positive view that as we age, we need to *better take care of energy*, cultivate it for the precious resource it is. That means a variety of things that we will cover this month.

How has your energy changed over the years?

[YOUR JOURNAL]

RECOVERY RITUALS

What happens when energy is depleted? Do you act, think or feel differently in these moments? Also, consider the people around you. When a work colleague seems low on energy, or a family member, what does that look like?

A lack of energy may result in a lack of interest or motivation, even apathy in extreme cases, which can affect a range of areas from performance to relationships.

Do you have any personal recharge rituals?

Perhaps it's getting into nature, exercise, social contact, calling a loved one, listening to music, having a bath.

Think about whether you need any of these today.

Think if you might suggest them to others.

MANAGE ENERGY, NOT TIME

was inspired early in my journey by the Corporate Athlete methodology. The key takeaway of that methodology is the call to *manage energy, not time*. This targets the world of work but can just as easily be applied to other parts of our lives.

We tend to focus on the quantitative stuff, the minutes and hours we're spending on things and, while measuring time spent is important, we must also consider the quality of those minutes and hours. What type of energy is going in and how does that input impact the output?

The right energy elevates the way we experience time by bringing clarity, fresh ideas, reward, and satisfaction—as opposed to just getting things done.

As you move through your day today (or reflect on the day that has passed), how might you better manage it by focusing on energy rather than time?

ENERGY SOURCES

The Corporate Athlete methodology is based on different sources of energy, represented as a hierarchy that builds up to a spiritual capacity and echoes the work of Abraham Maslow's hierarchy of human needs.

Physical capacity is at the base. This builds endurance and promotes mental and emotional recovery.

Emotional capacity is the second level. This creates the internal climate that drives an ideal performance state.

Mental capacity comes next. This focuses physical and emotional energy on the task at hand.

Spiritual capacity is at the top of the hierarchy. This provides a powerful source of motivation, determination and endurance.

Where are you on the above? Draw the hierarchy in the space below and add some notes on your present state.

DIMENSIONS OF ENERGY

We might try and increase our energy if it is low. So, often, we think of energy in terms of high or low. Yet that isn't the only dimension.

Anger and passion are both high energy states but they are very different from one another. Energy can also be considered as positive or negative.

This gives us the four energy quadrants as represented in a 2 x 2 matrix: high and positive (sometimes called the performance zone), high and negative (survival zone), low and positive (recovery zone), and low and negative (burnout zone).

Draw the matrix below. Where did you spend your time today?

EXCESS ENERGY

The original Corporate Athlete work by Jim Loehr and Tony Schwartz traces its evolution from coaching professional athletes. Schwartz subsequently accelerated its application within the corporate world through The Energy Project.

One of their recent areas of development is in regards to the tipping point for our own areas of strength. When excess energy is applied to an area we consider positive and valuable, that trait can then turn negative and be a detriment to ourselves and others.

For example, self-control overused can become rigidity. Tenacity becomes ruthlessness, courage becomes recklessness, and honesty becomes cruelty.

Take care with the energy you apply to your strengths today. Remain mindful of the need for balance.

PANDEMIC FATIGUE

An extreme low energy state for a prolonged period of time enters the realm of fatigue. I've experienced this now and then in my life on both a physical level (for example after a long athletics season), a mental level (upon submitting my Doctoral thesis), and an emotional level (positively, after the birth of my son).

If attention isn't paid to addressing fatigue it can result in burnout, which is a much more complicated issue to resolve.

I think we've all experienced some form of fatigue since early 2020 when the pandemic changed the world forever. Pandemic fatigue has been blamed for a rising number of cases of social disobedience (which in turn prolong the pandemic, and resultant fatigue) since people become fed up with restrictions and rules, becoming reckless.

What seems to impact us most is the lack of a finish line. At least for the moment, many of us don't have a set date for when we can resume many of the activities we once enjoyed freely before the pandemic, like travelling or seeing family members.

Acknowledging this fatigue is an important first step. Give yourself space today to think about how your energy level has been affected by the uncertainty caused by the pandemic.

SURVIVING TO THRIVING

I f there's one word that has been used almost excessively in recent years within the context of wellbeing, it is *thriving*. This is thanks to a variety of factors including Arianna Huffington's 'Thrive Global' consultancy and a general increase in interest within the field of wellbeing.

And the global pandemic gave further energy to the everyday use of 'thrive'—for example, some of the client programs we designed in Barcelona use the 'Surviving to Thriving' term.

Some days (and I think we've all had many of them as of late), there seems to be only just enough energy to get by. Survival mode.

But how do we move beyond that, to feeling that we are truly thriving in life?

What is it you need?

FLOURISHING AND LANGUISHING

T hough thriving has long been used in academic circles, particularly within the field of positive psychology, the more commonly used term is *flourishing*. The Harvard Human Flourishing Program defines the term as *"A state in which all aspects of a person's life are good."*

The American Sociology and Psychology Professor Corey Keyes considered the different aspects of a person's life within his Mental Health Continuum model. Looking at areas of wellbeing in the emotional, psychological, and social spaces, the model places people on a scale from languishing to flourishing.

Languishing has been a common response to the global pandemic. It's not quite at the danger of burnout or depression, but not moving forward with life either. A state of limbo, perhaps.

Where do you think you are you on the scale? Consider first the three areas of wellbeing in Keyes's model.

- *Emotional*:
  My overall happiness and interest in life.
- *Social*:
  How I connect to my wider community and society at large.
- *Psychological*:
  How I develop and grow as a person.

THE MENTAL HEALTH CONTINUUM MODEL

The Mental Health Continuum Model (MHC-SF) contains the following 14 items. Whether you are languishing or flourishing comes down to the frequency of the following items *during the past month*. How often did you feel:

1. happy?
2. interested in life?
3. satisfied with life?
4. that you had something important to contribute to society?
5. that you belonged to a community?
6. that our society is a good place, or is becoming a better place, for all people?
7. that people are basically good?
8. that the way our society works makes sense to you?
9. that you liked most parts of your personality?
10. good at managing the responsibilities of your daily life?
11. that you had warm and trusting relationships with others?
12. that you had experiences that challenged you to grow and become a better person?
13. confident to think or express your own ideas and opinions?
14. that your life has a sense of direction or meaning to it?

Response options: A 6-point scale—0: never, 1: once or twice, 2: about once a week, 3: about 2–3 times/week, 4: almost every day, 5: everyday.

continued to next page

continued from previous page

Total score: Questions are summed, yielding a total score ranging from 0 to 70. Higher scores indicate greater levels of positive wellbeing.

Flourishing mental health is defined by reporting one or more of questions 1–3 or six or more of questions 4–14 as experienced "every day" or "almost every day."

MODELS OF WELLBEING

The Mental Health Continuum Model discussed on April 10th and 11th includes three different areas of wellbeing. Wellbeing models have proliferated in recent years as a result of increasing attention in academia and business. I've reviewed dozens of these models in preparation for *The Daily Reset*, from corporations to wellbeing consultancies, academic and government studies to charities and foundations.

The main areas of wellbeing that I think we should pay attention to are the sources of energy. Which do you need to work on?

PHYSICAL WELLBEING

MENTAL WELLBEING

SPIRITUAL WELLBEING

CAREER AND FINANCIAL WELLBEING

SOCIAL AND SOCIETAL WELLBEING

DO SOMETHING

When we feel bad, low on energy let's say, we tend not to do anything. And, unsurprisingly, nothing changes. When we do anything, even something small, change occurs.

We feel a bit better.

If you're not feeling great today, do something.

MANAGING ENERGY AT WORK

We're working longer than ever before. More hours in the day, more days in the week, more weeks in the year, (not to mention more years in our life). Studies show that during the pandemic the average working day increased by as much as 30% for some people.

So how do you manage your energy at work?

In an interview with *Fortune* magazine in 2007, former CEO and Chairman of Procter & Gamble AG Lafley described how he changed his approach to work.

> I'd be up in the morning between 5 and 5:30.
> I'd work out and be at my desk by 6:30 or 7,
> drive hard until about 7pm, then go home,
> take a break with my wife, Margaret, and be
> back at it later that evening. I was just grinding
> through the day. Now I work really hard for an
> hour or an hour and a half. Then I take a break.
> I walk around and chit-chat with people. It can
> take five or 15 minutes to recharge. It's kind of
> like the interval training that an athlete does.

Watch out if you find yourself grinding through today. How can you change your schedule to open up moments that allow you to periodically recharge?

SUSTAINABLE PERFORMANCE

When I began my career in workplace wellbeing 20 years ago, wellbeing was almost exclusively viewed as a compromise on getting things done.

The work of the Corporate Athlete used a different word: performance. So, rather than being perceived as about doing less work, the performance view of wellbeing allows us to think about working *smarter*.

However, in many organizations the pendulum has swung too far and the result is an entire industry of 'peak performance' vendors who use the tools of wellbeing to squeeze even more out of the workforce. Wellbeing may be more present, but if the ultimate intent is simply performance, company culture remains a barrier to a true positive, empathetic, and human organization.

There can be residual benefits to this focus, but the end result is often a highly engaged workforce (good) that is close to burnout (bad). That situation cannot last, the sustainability of performance must be taken into account.

Performance is great. Just don't take it too far.

Think about sustainability.

ENERGY AUDITS

"You can't manage what you can't measure."

Peter Drucker

Try an energy audit today.

Write it down below or use another way to track such as Excel. Maybe you continue the tracking for a week.

Check in with yourself every hour. What's your level of energy (low or high) and nature of that energy (positive or negative). Perhaps add some notes on the context at that time.

THE DAILY RHYTHM

Your energy will fluctuate today. Just like every day.

Feeling sleepy after lunch? The nap zone is a part of our natural human biology—the *circadian rhythm* which dictates our daily pattern. A typical time for that dip is 3pm, when you might benefit from some reenergising actions (or just take the nap!) and is the time of day when most car accidents occur. The corresponding dip is 3am and this is when, rather depressingly, most suicides occur.

Being aware of our higher energy states is just as important as knowing when the dips occur. What did your energy audit from April 15th tell you? When are you most alert? Doing your best work? Coming up with your best ideas?

Aligning activities with your energy is essential. An easy example: is responding to emails or doing administrative tasks really the best use of your energy highpoint for the day?

Use your energy wisely.

A 24.5-HOUR SOCIETY

T he origins of circadian rhythm science can be traced to the fields of chronobiology and chronobiochemistry and, in particular, to the early 20th century German botanists who formed a leading school of thought in these areas.

The word circadian is taken from the Latin circa *dia*, meaning "around a day." Our circadian rhythm lasts about 24.5 hours (normalised to the 24-hour day with the help of the sun) during which time our body temperature will rise and fall together with various other body functions. This internal clock pre-empts each part of the day. It ensures that sleep, wakefulness, alertness, and various hormones will be at their most suitable levels.

As we move further and further into a 24-hour society—80% of the world's population lives in the haze of perpetual glow in the hours of darkness—perhaps it's worthwhile considering the need to align to these natural rhythms. There are increasing reports of the damage we are doing from being *always on*. For example, an estimated one billion birds die each year from flying into buildings, with light pollution thought to be the major factor.

If we're always on, without any reset, our energy will eventually wane and disappear. How can you better tune in to your own rhythms and those around you?

THE 16-SECOND CURE

The creators of the Corporate Athlete methodology focused much of their original work in peak performance on elite tennis players.

One key research insight came after video analysis on the difference between good professional tennis players and the standout champions of the game. They found that the champions would take just a little bit more time to fully recover between points. This increased time was small (there is a maximum of 30 seconds between points) yet consistent across all cases. They would ask for the towel to rub down, even if not strictly necessary, or take a few seconds extra on ball selection.

This energy management or reset allowed them to maintain performance in a long match and led Jim Loehr and his team to develop a method for deep recovery between points. Termed "the 16-second cure," they worked with players to develop a ritual of recovery in the short time available, combining physical actions with mental cues to move their attention fully to winning the next point.

What could be your 16-second cure today?

MICRO-BREAKS

Micro-breaks are any brief activity that help to break up the monotony of energy draining tasks. They can last a few seconds or even several minutes and involve anything from making a cup of tea to stretching or watching a music video.

Though the breaks are tiny, they can have a disproportionately powerful impact—studies have shown that they can improve our ability to concentrate, change the way we see our jobs, and even improve health and safety for office-based workers.

Research from Sooyeol Kim and colleagues in 2018 found the most effective micro-breaks come in three categories:

- *Relaxation* (for example, stretching, looking out the window or any activity where your cognitive load decreases)
- *Social* (for example, chatting with coworkers on non-work topics or messaging or calling friends)
- *Cognitive* (for example, reading books or newspapers or browsing the web for entertainment such as watching a funny video).

What can you try today?
When do you need the micro-break?
How long will it last?

SOME SOMATICS?

Throughout *The Daily Reset* we emphasise the importance of our physical selves for wellbeing. The movement and exercise themes in January and July take a deep dive in this space and I hope that the reset of the pandemic makes more people re-discover their physical selves.

Somatics is a field of practice that connects the physical, mental, emotional and spiritual. Pilates, the Alexander technique, Qi Gong and more broadly dance, may all be associated with the area. Pay closer attention during movement, for example, when rising from a chair, to develop better somatic awareness.

Whichever way you practice, and without overcomplicating matters, how might you move to best connect body and mind? There lies a powerful source of energy.

FOUR SPACES

A thletes are well versed in the art of active recovery. Sometimes the best thing to do is light exercise—allowing oxygen-rich blood to travel through the body—and help repair any little niggles or injuries.

I've found this to be true by experiencing the other side too. Sometimes after doing *less*—oversleeping, having a nap, not moving, a beach day on vacation—I feel *worse* in terms of my energy. Yet depending on the context, doing nothing might be exactly what you need.

On one dimension the means of improving energy may be therefore be via active or passive recovery.

The other dimension regards the physical and mental. Many athletes may be in perfect shape physically but at certain times, for example at the end of a long season, they are simply mentally exhausted. This can be true for us too. How do you feel at the end of a long project or when a personal issue keeps popping up over an extended period of time?

Four spaces, which can be represented on a 2 x 2 matrix, to consider to reenergise: active, passive, physical, mental.

What are you most in need of today?

ADDING AND SUBTRACTING

As you go through your day today, your energy will go up and it will go down. It can be positive or it can be negative. We've covered that concept already this month. But do you know why?

Your natural energy cycles are a big part of this, of course— as are the choices you make regarding how you move and what you eat. A final consideration is in regards to whom you interact with and the things you do.

Some people will drain your energy. Maybe they're always complaining or display a particular trait you dislike. I think we should always be fair and compassionate with others but if there is an individual who consistently lowers your energy, watch the amount of time you spend with them. Spend more time with those who always increase or improve your energy, for example through an enjoyable conversation.

The work you do may also be energising or it may be de-motivating. We might not always have the luxury of choosing our work but I hope at least you have a mix of these two extremes.

For today, think on the things that add and subtract energy in your life.

When thinking about people what behaviours do they show?

When thinking about work what conditions are present?

DON'T FORGET THE CALORIES!

The calorie has a bad reputation. But it's simply a measure of energy, specifically the amount of heat needed to raise the temperature of a gram of water by one degree. The 'big' calorie that we see on nutrition labels, or kCal, is the amount of heat needed to cause the same increase in one kilogram of water.

We need energy to move, think, and simply stay alive. The brain consumes most of that energy—around 20% in spite of only accounting for 2% of overall body weight. That means during a typical day, a person uses about 320 calories just to think. Hard thinking will require more calories but—before you get too excited—the difference is too small to make any kind of difference in weight management.

The simple takeaway: if you want to continue moving and thinking well throughout the day, don't forget to eat!

DOOMSCROLLING

Are you a slave to the smartphone? How much power does social media have over you?

Your mobile device can be a significant drain of both your time and energy. *Doomscrolling*—spending an excessive amount of time on social feeds—often makes us feel worse and yet, even when we are aware of this, it is hard to stop. If you find this to be an issue today, make an attempt to take back some control. Try the following:

- Turn off all push notifications in your settings. So, no red bubble notifications, sounds, or banners. You open the apps when you want to.
- Create some friction by hiding or deleting addictive apps. For example, when placed in a sub-folder or away from the front screen it will take extra steps to open them so you won't do it automatically and mindlessly.
- Have a clear simple front screen with no apps, preferably with a calming image. Tidy and organise all apps.
- Change your phone to greyscale. The lack of colour dramatically reduces the device's power to trigger your attention.
- Put your phone on airplane mode when you want to concentrate for a period of time, or place it in a drawer and out of sight all together.

ENERGY IS CONTAGIOUS

When I first became a dog-owner, I was puzzled by something one of my friends did. When he saw my young dog he would immediately jump up and down in a frenzied state, at which point the dog would do the same. He would then remark, *"Wow, Steven, your dog is crazy!"*

Pretty obvious to most people I think, but the levels to which a dog can pick up on your emotional state is remarkable. As I got to know my dog better and spend time with her, I realised how attuned she was to my own emotions, sometimes even more than I was myself. For example, there were times that I'd only become aware I was anxious when I saw that mirrored in her behaviour.

Do you remember the last time you had exciting news to share? How did the person you told react? You probably found that they became excited and enthused too. Energy is contagious.

This of course can be good or bad. A bad mood can similarly affect others as well as a state of low energy or apathy.

Be mindful of the energy you bring to other people. And dogs.

YOU HAVE A RESPONSIBILITY

ndiana University Health in the United States have a sign on their doors visible to people entering the building:

> *Please take responsibility for the energy you bring into this space. Your words matter. Your behaviors matter. Our patients and our teams matter.*
>
> *Take a slow, deep breath and make sure your energy is in check before entering.*
>
> *Thank you.*

!!!

I was taking a micro-break and playing with my six-year-old son. We were rearranging letters he had as part of a toy to make words and he asked me what an exclamation mark meant. I instinctively responded that it gives extra energy to a word.

I then remembered the American neo-punk band *!!!* (pronounced tch, tch, tch) who were certainly high-energy in concert the few times I saw them perform live.

How will you add an ! to a part of your life today?

PASSION

What do you love doing? Or what did you love doing when you were younger?

Whatever it is, you probably feel a warm glow just thinking about it. Passion is hugely energising, especially when we indulge it. Unfortunately, many people leave their own special interests and passions on the side of their increasingly busy life-path where other commitments, including work and family, often take precedence. We even feel guilty and selfish when considering doing something just for ourselves. Yet, reconnecting with your passions is perhaps the most unselfish thing you can do. Others, both at home and in the workplace, will get the best out of you.

Sharing your passions with a family member or work colleague can increase their benefit and when you take the time to uncover passions in your team, it will increase engagement and performance as a whole. Work is no longer about the quantity of time put into it but, rather, the engagement and the quality of energy we brought to it.

In the best cases, passion may also align with purpose but, just like purpose, it might take some searching to find it.

Today, think about what you love. Go do it.

BREATHE IT IN

Wim Hof is the iceman. He is a hugely inspiring pioneer who has confounded scientists for years with his ability to withstand extreme cold. He advocates cold exposure as a means of reducing stress and improving energy. At the core of his method is a specific type of breathing. Get comfortable and try the following:

30–40 Deep Breaths
Close your eyes and try to clear your mind. Be conscious of your breath, and try to fully connect with it. Inhale deeply through the nose or mouth, and exhale unforced through the mouth. Fully inhale through the belly, then chest and then let go unforced. Repeat this 30 to 40 times in short, powerful bursts. You may experience light-headedness, and tingling sensations in your fingers and feet. These side effects are completely harmless.

The Hold
After the last exhalation, inhale one final time, as deeply as you can. Then let the air out and stop breathing. Hold until you feel the urge to breathe again.

Recovery Breath
When you feel the urge to breathe again, draw one big breath to fill your lungs. Feel your belly and chest expanding. When you are at full capacity, hold the breath for around 15 seconds, then let go. That completes round number one. This cycle can be repeated 3–4 times without interval. After having completed the breathing exercise, take your time to bask in the bliss. This calm state is highly conducive to meditation—don't hesitate to combine the two.

A LIMITED RESOURCE

Energy is a precious resource. It's also limited.

This is true of both ourselves and the world that surrounds us. Taking care of how we create energy and how we use energy, being more mindful of it, will improve our own lives and the life of the planet.

Today, this mindful view of energy might mean you do nothing or spring to action. It might mean you focus on the things you can control or try and influence the behaviour of those around you.

Remain mindful of energy. Pay attention today and every day.

MAY

MINDFULNESS

TIME

Growing up in Scotland, I loved the month of May. It seemed to be the first month of the year that we actually saw the sun! And with it came the promise of the end of the school term and beyond that, an endless summer. The days were long, and getting longer.

As an adult living in Spain, it's still a special month. It's just that it seems to pass by more quickly each time.

Studies on the perception of time have found that as we age, we feel time is passing at a faster rate. Our brain encodes new experiences, but not familiar ones, into memory, and our retrospective perception of time is based on how many new memories we create over a certain period. In other words, the more new memories we build during a holiday, the longer that trip will seem in hindsight. Another theory on the passage of time relates it as a function of the time we have already lived. So, for a ten-year-old, a year is 10% of their life and to a 20-year-old it is 5%. Using this logic, the following time periods would have the same perception: 5–10, 10–20, 20–40 and 40–80.

How do we slow it down?

Mindfulness.

[YOUR JOURNAL]

55 SECONDS

Give me a minute of your time, please. You might want to read it through first, or ask someone to read it to you—you'll understand why after the first line.

- Close your eyes.
- First, be conscious of your breathing. In and out. Your chest rising and falling.
- Now bring your attention to your physical self. Your body, perhaps sitting on a chair, or standing. Feel your head, your neck. Your shoulders. Your back. Your legs. Your feet. If they're not already flat, put your feet flat on the ground.
- Nothing to do. If any thoughts come in to your mind, let them come, and let them go. I'm going to leave you like that, for just a short while.
  [55 seconds]
- Keeping your eyes closed, again be conscious of your breathing, in and out. Bring your attention now, again, to your body. Your head, chest, back and those feet, flat on your part of the Earth that we all share.
- And when you're ready, open your eyes.

I've run this mindful minute several hundred times in the past ten years to thousands of people. Maybe you can try it today.

The trying is key. As with every theme in *The Daily Reset,* we learn and develop much more through doing. Especially this month, you will understand the nudges much more deeply if you practice mindfulness. Start with these 55 seconds.

KRONOS AND KAIROS

"The shortening of the years as we grow
older is due to the monotony of the memory's
content and the consequent simplification
of the backward-glancing view. Emptiness,
monotony, and familiarity are what make time
shrivel up."

William James

The Ancient Greeks had two concepts of time: Kronos, the conventional measure in minutes and hours, but also Kairos, which was the experience of that time.
Bring more Kairos into your life today.

MINDFUL OR MINDLESS?

Mindfulness has enjoyed significant attention in recent years because it is an antidote to *mindlessness*, a state that has taken over many areas of our lives.

During much of our day we operate on 'autopilot'. As discussed in the month of February, we need automaticity in our lives. Automatic behaviour, including decision making, saves us time and energy, allowing us to get things done. But it can go too far, and that can happen to negative affect in different parts of our lives.

In the workplace, we accumulate skills and knowledge with experience—and operating in that 'autopilot' mode could be considered a sign of competence. Yet sooner or later, optimum efficiency becomes outdated. We need to break apart the patterns of the existing way of doing things and try new things.

At work, but also in many other areas of our lives, we are *addicted to busy* or some other form of chaos. This promotes mindless behaviour and automatic triggers throughout the day.

Technology, and the addictive aspects of social media in particular, has also instilled in us an automatic mindless behaviour.

As you go through your day today, automatic behaviour will serve an important purpose. Just try and bring your attention to that automation and ask if it is indeed valuable, or simply mindless.

DON'T KILL BOREDOM

"The cure for boredom is curiosity."

Dorothy Parker

I remember as a young child, particularly stuck inside on rainy days, remarking to my parents that I was bored. They would reply to me—'that's because you're boring'. A tad harsh, I think!

In any case I'm not sure that boredom exists anymore, at whatever age. We have created a society of constant entertainment and stimuli and try to 'kill' boredom at the first sign of its appearance.

Yet, studies have found that boredom serves an important purpose. It is a necessary pre-condition for creativity and curiosity, of understanding the best way forward. On reflection, I think my parents were trying to say to me it was important to be comfortable with myself and my own mind, and to figure out my own path forward.

If you find yourself getting bored today, consider it unexpected space rather than unused space. Don't automatically kill it. Stay with it, observe it, experience it, feel it. And think about what it's telling you.

MINDFULNESS IS NOT JUST MEDITATION

O f course, an important element of mindfulness is the 'not doing', just being in the present moment. This is what many of us call meditation.

Yet we can also apply mindfulness to our doing. The actions that make up our daily lives—walking, eating, showering, talking, listening. The mundane and everyday as well as the special.

For example, researchers at the University of California San Francisco found the benefits of an 'awe walk' for emotional well-being. The research was focused on 52 older adults who were asked to take at least one 15-minute walk each week for eight weeks.

They reported increased positive emotions and less distress in their daily lives. This shift was reflected in 'selfies' that participants took on their weekly walks, in which an increasing focus on their surroundings rather than themselves was paralleled by measurably broader smiles by the end of the study.

Be it a walk, or something else you do every day, how can you bring more mindfulness to your actions?

MINDFULNESS
HAS MANY BENEFITS

M indfulness can be defined as 'as a moment-to-moment awareness of our experience without judgment'.

It is a state of being. It is not meditation, if meditation is indeed used to be mindful, but a result of it. Brain imaging research even shows that mindfulness changes the brain. It is well supported in numerous studies to have significant benefits, including:

- Reduced rumination,
- Reduced stress,
- Better working memory,
- Better focus,
- Less emotional reactivity,
- More cognitive flexibility and better cognitive performance,
- More satisfying relationships,
- Stronger morality and intuition,
- A stronger immune system.

I think we can all do with some of these benefits in our life—so give mindfulness a go.

MINDFULNESS
IS NOT PERFECT

t is important to remember that mindfulness is not perfect. It is not, on its own, the answer to all our challenges in life.

Amidst the global clamour to implement mindfulness practice, some researchers highlight the counter case. Some of this is linked to how we have implemented it in modern society. In his book *McMindfulness: How Mindfulness Became the New Capitalist Spirituality*, management professor Ronald Purser describes how modern practice has become divorced from the original Buddhist teachings and that it has become just another "stripped-down, DIY, self-help technique."

Other recent research has even found mindfulness to promote more selfish behaviour and can also lead to increased anxiety as well as trigger panic attacks.

Just like everything in life there's no silver bullet, and mindfulness is no exception. It's one of a variety of tools we can use.

In fact, you have 366 of them in your hands right now.

ARE YOU SITTING COMFORTABLY?

I f we think of mindfulness or indeed any form of meditation, our mind may conjure up the famous image of the cross-legged person, eyes closed, fingers and thumbs touching. The lotus pose.

You don't need to do that.

You can, of course. Personally, I've never found it the most comfortable position—and that comfort is the key. Adopt a position, preferably sitting, in which you are comfortable and able, if you wish, to keep that same position for an extended period of time.

Some people have a meditation cushion. For me, it is important to have my feet flat on the ground.

Do whatever works for you. Before you begin, get comfortable.

VIPASSANA

Some people do indeed manage to extend their meditation longer than the 55 seconds I advocated at the beginning of the month. Have you maintained practice?

A Vipassana is a ten-day silent retreat in which one learns the ancient techniques of meditation practice. Vipassana means to see things as they really are and it was first taught in India more than 2,500 years ago as a remedy for life's problems.

Courses can be found around the world and they are always completely free, with the costs being met from donations by people who have previously attended a course.

Days pass in total silence, with even direct eye contact between residents discouraged. Apart from eating and sleeping, time is either spent in silent meditation or performing the simplest of chores required for the retreat to function.

Think about your life. Sometimes even one hour in complete silence, with no technology and no direct contact with the outside world is beyond us. Now think of a full day. Now ten days.

It's no wonder that people come back from a Vipassana, quite simply, renewed.

GOING LONG

'm not sure how feasible a Vipassana (see yesterday's nudge) is for my life today, but it got me thinking: what's the longest I've meditated for?

Ten minutes has been the de facto duration over the years, with that sometimes reaching 30–45 in a group session. And so, I tested my own limits before writing this entry: 90 minutes.

As with my previous books in the summers of 2014 and 2017, *The Daily Reset* is the result of an intense writing period over several weeks. The final week in particular (for the first draft manuscript) was intense and exhausting. I tried those 90 minutes right at the end.

It was *very* hard, I'll admit it. But also, hugely restorative.

It made me realise the layers and space I have inside myself, something admittedly I've thought of before, but the longer you meditate the more you peel this back. It fed my curiosity. Maybe one day I will try a Vipassana.

What's the longest you've meditated for? Maybe it's worth trying something just a little longer?

PAST, PRESENT, AND FUTURE

A common part of guided practice during mindfulness meditation will be moving your finger to one side or another, say, on your leg, when you notice your attention leaving the present moment. For example, if you think of a memory or something you have to do later that day or week.

And this is the typical way we live our lives. Think about what it's like when talking with friends. We often recall good times or look ahead to what we are excited (or worried) about happening in the future. Essentially, we spend much of our time planning our busy days and reflecting on the mistakes we have made. It's no wonder it's not as easy as it sounds to be fully in the moment.

Create more moments in your day when you are fully present. Don't just think about what you're doing next, or what you've just done.

Think about the conversations you have. Which timeframe is the focus of that conversation? Make reference to the things that surround you. In a meeting, lead by example by leaving all technology out of sight and ask for clarification on what someone is saying.

The past and the future will be a significant element of your day today. Just don't forget about the present.

PAYING ATTENTION

The artist Jackson Pollock received a letter from his father that read:

> "The secret of success is to be fully awake to everything about you."

Observation is a key method in the field of design. I remember reading an article by IDEO's Executive Chair, Tim Brown, about the value of conducting observation.

He wrote that once a day, we should stop and take a second look at some ordinary situation that you would normally look at only once (or not at all)—as if you were a detective at a crime scene. He said that by feeding our curiosity and immersing ourselves in the "super-normal" we develop incredibly rich insights into the unwritten rules that guide us through life.

Brown concludes that good design thinkers observe and great design thinkers observe the ordinary.

How can you elevate yourself today from good to great? Perhaps include notes from your observations below:

DO SOMETHING DIFFERENT

As we age, we tend to settle into the same routines. Of doing, thinking and behaving. There's less *difference*. Do something different today. Anything. Do something for the first time. Break out of your usual patterns. Ask yourself whether you are on a journey or are you in the same space countless times? Try noticing something for the first time. New things will start to present themselves.

Bring an element of difference today.

COLOURS

Think of a colour that is not blue or green.

Now look out the window and find as many things as possible with your chosen colour.

Better still, do this when you have a view, perhaps high up over a large area of land, or even on a walk.

This tactic will help if you ever feel overwhelmed. It will help you be present. It will help you to be mindful.

MINDFUL WALKING

Universitas Telefónica is an incredible place. For a decade this corporate campus in the middle of a forest 30 kilometres north of Barcelona hosted several thousand busy professionals from around the world to experience a week of deep transformation.

I was lucky enough to teach a lot of classes there. The classroom-based work was great but what I most enjoyed was getting out into that forest.

One of the activities that I led was a mindfulness walk. I say led, but it was actually led by my sheepdog Harry. She would accompany us around a loop of the forest providing an important anchor for the group and reminder to remain mindful, especially if there was a temptation to pull out the mobile phone.

Dogs don't think about the past or the future. They engage all of their senses in their immediate and present surroundings.

Be more dog today.

MINDFUL STEPS (PART II)

"My home shall be open for the sun and the
wind and the voices of the sea—like a Greek
temple—and light, light, light everywhere!"

Axel Munthe

I've been very fortunate to vacation in Capri for the past 10 years. As well as the more typical vacation pursuits, I love to run and Capri is a paradise for running in nature with many challenging routes. The Phoenician Steps have been a particular focus since my first visit, not least because it's one of the first (truly amazing) things you see when you get off the funicular and arrive at Capri piazzetta.

However, for anyone with vertigo, like me, running those steps is a daunting prospect—several hundred steps in the side of the mountain rising over 200m in just 600m with sections near 50% incline. Built by the ancient Greeks, it was the only means of connecting Capri and Anacapri before the construction of the road in 1874.

I overthought it for years, turned back half-way up one year and finally did it in 2018. Contrary to all that overthinking, my main emotions during the ascent are deep calm and joy.

Things are never as bad as we make them out to be in our head.

Embrace your vulnerabilities.

Focus on one step at a time rather than being freaked out by the big picture.

FLORA AND FAUNA

Capri is a very glamorous island. It is well known for its superyachts, expensive shops, and fine dining. But it is much more than that.

What struck me immediately on my first visit was the island's immense natural beauty. The cliffs and the sea. The incredible sunsets. Intense purple Bougainvillea everywhere. Songs of birds I didn't recognise and which sounded as if they were truly celebrating a new day. Space and air and quiet.

Even writing these words transports me back there. And those things make me fully mindful when I am lucky enough to be there.

The natural world is an incredible source of mindfulness. And the deeper you are mindful the deeper the memories for you to use and call on anytime you need them.

FIVE SENSES

The Economist reported on the case of 62-year-old Larry in an edition during early 2021.

At the time of publication, Larry had been void of human contact for more than a year. Described as a "touchy-feely" person, he longs for casual platonic contact: hugs and handshakes, and lies in bed yearning to hold someone or be held, yet is deprived of all due to pandemic constraints. *The Economist* writers state that touch is "the only sense crucial to human survival."

Whereas the pandemic took away much of our exposure to touch, modern society in general has slowly but steadily taken away our exposure to all our senses, at least in a mindful way.

We have five senses:

- What we see.
- What we smell.
- What we hear.
- What we touch.
- What we taste.

How can you better engage all of these today?

If you do, you will enjoy a mindful day.

SIXTH SENSE

Close your eyes please.

Can you feel your heartbeat?

This is a simple test of assessing your *interoception*. A fast-moving area of study in neuroscience and psychology, it is the sense of what's going on in your body, based on signals sent from your internal organs to the brain.

Scientists are understanding this sixth sense has enormous impact on our wellbeing.

Try tuning in to your internal organs during mindfulness, and throughout the day. Itchiness, hunger, temperature, muscle tension or a clenching stomach, breathing, your beating heart. All are important signals.

Develop your sixth sense and you'll feel the benefit.

MINDFULNESS STARTS WITH THE BODY

Breathing is one of the first elements of mindfulness practice, particularly how that breathe moves through the body. A body scan is a practice that can help with being present and allow us to realise some of the benefits of mindfulness. It is relatively easy and you can spend a short or long time on it, bringing your attention to the many different parts of your body. A common practice is to start at one end of your body and move to the other—so top to toe or the other way.

Head, eyes, ears, neck, shoulders and at the other end heel, ankle, the individual toes of your foot. It can be a powerful experience to tune in to each of these body parts one at a time. Perhaps check how each is—maybe you find yourself with your shoulders raised, your forehead wrinkled or some pain in a part of your foot. A body scan will allow you to relax each of these body parts, observe any aches and pains, and improve the awareness of your physical self.

If you have just five minutes available, or a long fifty, close your eyes and try a body scan.

It's called *mind*fulness but, in many ways, it starts with the body. How can you build a stronger relationship between your body and your mind?

A MONK'S LIFE

"Life is really simple, but we insist on making
it complicated."

Confucius

A Buddhist monk will typically wake at 4:30am followed by early morning prayers or recitation and personal hygiene. They may then go to collect alms and return for breakfast. Learning takes up the rest of the morning with the main meal of the day around lunchtime, which for them is, typically the last meal of the day. More learning, prayers and meditation follow and then comes the afternoon when work is done for the physical upkeep of the monastery. Everyone is in bed by 7pm. Seven days a week, 365 (or 366) days a year.

Could you live such a life? I know I couldn't. But, still, maybe there are some elements of their experience we could adopt?

The last stretch of writing this book gave me some insight. Several days alone, mostly in silence, following a simple routine each day. Early to bed and early to rise. I wouldn't want that as my typical life but there was a pleasure and fullness in the simplicity and isolation, of observing the same patterns in the world around me each day, of appreciating the symmetry.

What monastic practices could you implement today? Decluttering? Listening without judgement? Learning something new? Taking on just one task at a time? Letting go of what you can't control?

We don't need to be a monk to be more monk.

A STOIC'S LIFE

"People look for retreats for themselves, in the country, by the coast, or in the hills. There is nowhere that a person can find a more peaceful and trouble-free retreat than in his own mind. So constantly give yourself this retreat, and renew yourself."

Marcus Aurelius

Whereas Buddhist monks typically live apart from normal life, the Stoics were known for being a part of it. Actually, they were right in the thick of the action and this helped shape the thinking of Stoic philosophy.

There was no more chaotic a place then (or even perhaps since) than Ancient Rome where Marcus Aurelius and other renowned Stoics like Seneca lived. Their philosophy was based on three main ideas: recognising that some things are in our control and others not, understanding that it's not things that upset us, but our judgments about these things, and that we must act with virtue (being a morally good person) at every moment.

If you find yourself in the middle of a chaotic day today, adopting these three ideas will help. Be more Stoic.

JOURNALING

*T*he *Daily Reset* is my journal. It is now your journal.
Numerous studies have found the practice of journaling to be hugely beneficial for mental health. I think it's important to find the style that suits you best. Maybe reading *The Daily Reset* and adding some notes now and again is enough. Maybe you want to go further with a dedicated, blank journal. Here are some considerations to get you started:

Identify a time and place where you will have the best chance of quiet time and some personal headspace.
For example, some people will do this at the very beginning or end of the day. Having the right frame of mind is important, so experiment with the time/place until you find one that suits you. Also try a relaxing ritual to prepare for the process below.

Have a pen and paper.
It is important to write down your thoughts, something that comes more naturally with a pen or pencil rather than a keyboard, or at least have the option of writing them down should you wish to do so. One word could be enough, or one page.

Consider your recent experiences, for example over the course of the previous day.
What went well? What didn't go so well? How did you feel?

With regular practice you may begin to identify patterns of behaviour and how other people and events affect you. Embrace the positive and don't hide from the negative—that is part of the learning, and value of journaling.

VISUALISATION

"If you can see it and believe it, it is a lot easier to achieve it."

Oprah Winfrey

Visualisation is a common technique used in sport. As a young athlete, I would implement some of the basics before a big race. It helped me deal with nerves and any unexpected occurrences during competition. It helped me focus on the things I could control and let go of the things I couldn't. Ultimately, it helped me keep my cool and have the best chance of winning.

While visualisation is not mindfulness in that it takes us away from the present moment, it is a type of meditation that connects you with mind and improves the mind-body connection that can improve your life.

The interesting thing about the mind is that it has a difficult time distinguishing between reality and imagination. The same neural and biological processes take place for both.

Studies show that just by visualising something, the greater the likelihood that it will actually happen. For example, a study of job interview candidates found that the people who had prepared by visualising success were actually three times more likely to get the job.

What do you want to happen? Visualise it happening!

DELIBERATE PRACTICE

The more we do something, the better we get. Right?
Not quite.

In order to improve, we must elevate practice to something called *deliberate practice*. This involves bringing a higher level of focus to the thing we are doing, rather than *just* the doing. This involves a higher level of awareness of the specific components of a skill we're aiming to improve and the exact steps we need to take to do that.

Is there something in your life you want to be better at? Doing it more is obviously the place to start, the practice. Then also think about adding the following elements:

- Break down the overall thing into constituent parts,
- Measure your performance on these parts, ideally with feedback in the moment,
- Enlist a coach to be part of the process, to observe and give feedback,
- Know that deliberate practice is hard and will stretch you,
- Design action plans to address your weaknesses,
- Strive for progress to give you the energy to keep going.

This is doing, but *mindful* doing.

FLOW

A term first coined by the Hungarian psychologist Mihály Csíkszentmihályi, *flow* is the state of complete immersion in an activity, in which we are fully engaged and fulfilled.

Flow allows us to attain high performance, be the best version of ourselves, and allow us to maximise happiness and wellbeing. Often associated with artists and athletes, who do their best work when 'in the zone', flow has been identified by researchers to exist in a variety of activities around the world.

Flow is characterized by both the high skill level used and challenge level faced. If we are in flow, we are therefore *stretched* and using all our abilities to meet the challenge at hand. Flow may arise from practice, but it goes beyond practice in a demonstration of the thing we were perhaps born to master, it is our purpose.

Flow can also take us away from the physical self. According to Csikszentmihalyi, when total immersion takes place, time, food, and ego all disappear. In my own experiences with flow, in both my sporting and teaching activities, it feels as if I detach from what I'm doing and am able to become an observer of myself and the situation.

I think flow is therefore simultaneously the doing and the not doing. Where practice is elevated to a level of simply being.

Have you experienced flow?

TUMULTUOUS IMPERCEPTIBILITY

Mindfulness helps you appreciate balance and contrast in order to make sense of paradox.

I was lucky enough to write part of *The Daily Reset* on the paradise island of Formentera in Spain. I would get up early while my family was still sleeping and write for an hour on the beach. I would then finish with a short meditation.

During one of those meditations, my mind came up with the term *tumultuous imperceptibility* to describe how I was experiencing my current environment.

It was tumultuous—the crashing of the waves, the immense power of the rising sun. Noise and light and heat.

At the same time, it was imperceptible. I was tuning in to the small degrees of movement of the tides and the sun as it moved across my face. I also tuned in to the imperceptibility of my *self*—my heartbeat, my skin, my internal organs.

Does that make sense? Perhaps it does only to me, but practicing mindfulness frequently will allow you to tune in to your specific world and make more sense of it.

Come up with your own way of tuning into the world, with words, or none at all.

DAYS AND WEEKS

When I delivered programs at Universitas Telefónica in Barcelona, it was often an exhausting experience. I would arrive to campus on Monday morning for a reception that evening with up to 180 participants from all over the world. Classes would start early the next day and run until Friday lunchtime. Activities would take place after classes finished, followed by dinner at a very Spanish hour. My day could stretch from a 7am pre-breakfast run to a midnight after-dinner cocktail. During that week, it seemed we were always *on*.

What particularly struck me was the feeling that came over me during Friday lunch when we celebrated another successful week of transformation. It all seemed to have passed in a flash.

This is when I came up with the phrase: *The days are long but the weeks are short.*

If you feel your day stretching out and even find yourself complaining about its interminable nature, stop yourself. Don't try and escape from it. Go deeper. Immerse yourself in the experience.

Because when it's gone, you may wish for it to be back.

26,463 DAYS

"Either you run the day or the day runs you."
Jim Rohn

This is the average life expectancy for the world (72.5 years). In developed countries, it's a little higher at 80.5 years or 29,383 days.

It's not a lot, and if you're like me, you might be around half-way through.

Every day is worth it. Mindfulness will help you live it.

HEARTFULNESS

I first met Prashanth Vasu when teaching a group of McKinsey managers in Mumbai during summer 2018. He was warm, funny and cared deeply for the futures of the young managers in his care. He knew I integrated aspects of mindfulness in my Sustaining Executive Performance program and made a quiet suggestion that I also consider adding heartfulness, gifting me a copy of the book, *The Heartfulness Way* by Daaji.

Much has yet to be discovered on the exact link between the heart and the mind, and my own view of the heart over the years has been on a mostly biological level regarding exercise and fitness. Yet no consideration of the human heart can rest solely on the biological or neurological levels. A deeper, more emotional or perhaps spiritual consideration of who we are as human beings is necessary.

The Egyptians believed the heart to be the core of all that makes us uniquely human. They did all they could to preserve it during mummification. In contrast, they believed the brain to be superfluous. In many parts of modern culture, the heart represents the essence or centre of something and the means by which we give our all and are truly able to inspire others. It is the seat of what makes us human: compassion, joy, gratitude, and of course love.

I feel that is what heartfulness is. I say *feel* because it is a journey of understanding, separate from the thinking mind. A spiritual one. (Not a religious one necessarily but you can bring any religion you wish together with heartfulness). It regards a deeper self-awareness of who we are, the importance of practice over theory, and a path towards a better and truer version of ourselves.

However you decide to bring mindfulness into your life, if at all, bring your heart too.

NOTES ON YOUR JOURNEY THROUGH MINDFULNESS IN MAY:

JUNE

NUTRITION

EATING AND AGEING

[MY JOURNAL]

We are what we eat. It's a common refrain and I've been increasingly aware of it as I get older. As a young athlete, anything worked. It was all burned up in the furnace of training and the excess of youth. Yet many of those choices—the simple carbohydrates and starches that were the hallmark of those days—have not sat well with me in my late 30s and early 40s. Whereas a hangover in my early days came only after a big night out or celebration, I now seem to feel the same effects after a plate of crackers and parmesan! Indeed, I believe nutrition to be the biggest single factor in any growing sense of fragility I feel regarding my health as I enter middle age.

What about you? How have your eating habits, and how they make you feel, changed over the years?

[YOUR JOURNAL]

FUEL YOUR DAY

F ood is fuel. We are able to move and think during the day with the energy that food gives us.

How do you fuel yourself? A cartoon from *The New Yorker* several years ago showed two men in an office standing next to the coffee machine. One, pouring himself a cup, says to the other, "I try to keep my coffee buzz going till the martini buzz kicks in."

Fuel from food comes principally from calories and neither coffee nor alcohol are the best means of achieving that—coffee, on its own doesn't have any (or at most a negligible amount of) calories, and alcohol, though being one of the most effective means of triggering feel-good endorphins in humans, is actually a depressant.

In the 2008 Beijing Olympics, as he aimed to become the most successful swimmer of all time, Michael Phelps said he could do only three things: "eat, sleep, and swim". These actions are the 'holy trinity' of performance for any elite athlete.

I hope you get to do more than three things today! But consider how the food you eat provides fuel for what you want to do. How does your energy change as a result of your nutrition choices?

TAKE YOUR TIME

How fast do you eat?

Many of us eat too fast, either because we're hungry, busy, or doing other things at the same time. When we eat fast, we tend to overeat since we are not allowing the stomach the time it needs to send a signal to the brain to say it's full. Slowing down allows us to actually taste our food and better enjoy the experience of the meal.

How could you slow down? Try using chopsticks!

Estimates of the world population who use chopsticks range between 20–30%. When travelling in China, however, I have on occasion seen some hungry individual adding a spoon in one hand in addition to their chopsticks to increase their eating speed!

MINDFULNESS IS FOR EATING TOO

Here's a process we've used in hundreds of training programs over the years. If you don't like raisins you can substitute for something else, like a date or olive. Give it a go, and then try and apply some of the thinking to your meals.

- Take one raisin in your hand (don't eat it yet!)
- Observe the raisin as if you were seeing it for the first time. Think about where it came from—all of the processes and people that were involved so that this raisin is now in your hands.
- Feel its texture. Smell it.
- Close your eyes. Eat the raisin. Chew it. Taste it.

TRACKING WHAT YOU EAT

Being mindful of what we eat during the course of a day isn't always straight-forward. We lead ever-busier lives, grabbing something on the go or eating the first thing we see at home after a hard day.

Keeping a food diary is one of the first things a nutrition or fitness coach would ask a client to do. Try starting one today. You could also take a photo of everything you eat or, better still, note it below. Space permitting, give it a try on the pages which remain this month.

TRACKING WHEN YOU EAT

D o you eat breakfast? Or do you tend to skip it and normally eat large meals late at night? Hey, maybe you do both!

The issue of *when* we eat, like many areas of nutrition science, has conflicting views. Many believe a calorie to be a calorie regardless of when it is ingested, yet some recent studies do show an earlier consumption of calories to lead to weight loss.

Researchers at Northwestern University looked at late-night eating within the context of the circadian rhythm (our daily biological clock) to test their hypothesis on why night shift workers tend to be overweight. They found that late-night eating did indeed lead to weight gain.

Other research from Spain in the *International Journal of Obesity* found dieters who ate their main meal before 3pm to lose significantly more weight than those who ate later in the day. This held true even though the early eaters were eating roughly the same number of calories during the five-month weight-loss study as their night-owl counterparts.

Many experts believe the key is in aligning our eating habits with our sleep-wake cycle. Whatever the best strategy, start paying attention today to *when* you eat as well as what you eat.

INTERMITTENT FASTING

I n the end, all it took was leaving out the milk.

For years, my morning routine involved making coffee, specifically a *café con leche*. It was a key part of my morning. I had been aware of the growing science and support for intermittent fasting the past few years but couldn't quite bring myself to miss out on coffee to enable the fast. Then I found out black coffee has no calories (or at most such a negligible amount that it doesn't break your fast). And, I actually found myself enjoying the coffee more.

While the science around when we eat is conflicting, the support for intermittent fasting (sometimes called time-restricted eating) is clear: *eat in a smaller time window during your 24-hour day and you will improve health, and most probably lose weight.*

We live in an always-on society and part of that is we don't stop eating. Even if that food is healthy, we don't give our bodies a chance to do the other things it needs to do. It's always digesting food!

At least we don't eat when we're sleeping, but try and extend those hours to at least 12 of your daily 24 when you're not ingesting calories. Then try to expand that. Studies have found the 16–8 split to be most effective. This doesn't mean you can eat unlimited amounts of bad food in those eight hours, but give your body the chance to get to work during non-eating time.

- When did you start eating today?
- When did you stop?
- How could you reduce this window?

ASKING FOR SECONDS

"The first bite is the banquet. That's a Chinese rule. Every subsequent bite will be less good. It's never going to get better than that first bite, and once you realize that this is going downhill, you don't need to have the sixth or seventh bite."

Michael Pollan

Have you ever taken a photo of a plate of food you found particularly attractive? Perhaps you even posted it on Instagram?

Part of the enjoyment of eating is the anticipation, engaging all our senses—how it looks, how it smells. And oh, that first bite!

Contrast this with how you feel towards the end of a meal, particularly a large one.

Should you really ask for seconds today?

COOKING

'm no chef, but I love cooking.

I've found it to be a relaxing experience and sometimes combine it with listening to music, having a glass of wine, and socialising with friends and family—even getting them involved in the preparation of the meal. Numerous studies show that families who cook and eat together eat better.

I've learned a lot about food through the preparation of basic dishes and learning where it comes from, what happens when we use different methods of cooking, and what it does for us.

Cooking allows us to improve our nutritional health as well as our overall wellbeing—through socialisation, relaxation, exploring new things, and many other indirect aspects of good health.

Whether you're an accomplished chef or you find it impossible to successfully boil an egg, take some time today to prepare a meal.

Look up a new recipe to follow. Try and perfect *your* special dish.

HAUTE CUISINE

As someone who grew up with very simple food tastes, I find it funny that I came into immediate and frequent contact with the world of *haute cuisine* once I moved to Spain.

I won a running race in the Basque Country within a few months of arriving and the prize was dinner at *Arzak* where Chef Juan Mari and daughter Elena were kind and gracious hosts. I subsequently got to know the Roca brothers in Girona, the founders of *El Celler de Can Roca* (previously voted the best restaurant in the world), and had the distinct honour of having them cater my wedding.

I remain with mostly simple food preferences today but appreciate the huge amount we can learn from the world of fine dining—and its benefit for both us as individuals and the world around us.

This includes local sourcing of ingredients, growing our own food, top-to-tail eating (using all of the animal and minimising waste), small tasting portions and a more mindful approach eating. In general, a celebration of food as one of the finest human experiences.

We can all incorporate some of these haute cuisine principles in our own lives.

RAISING AWARENESS

You will eat today, just like every day. But, do you know where that food comes from?

After moving from Scotland to Spain in 2003, I was impacted greatly by actually seeing the animal in the market when shopping for meat. In Britain, as a whole, meat is very neatly packaged (go square sausage!) and even the wording in English doesn't always make it clear where it comes from, or which animal it is.

Sometimes we'd rather not know. Animal activists in recent years have tried to raise an awareness of what happens at the very earliest stages of the supply chain, which can make for grim reading, or viewing.

And it's not just animals. Other food that is made, as well as the transport of food around the world affects our own health and that of the planet.

Instilling a greater awareness in our children of the wider aspects of food, and of the great effort that takes place to ensure it arrives on our plate, is a worthy pursuit. The food industry could be used as a magnificent lens for educating young people in so many different fields, from supply chain to engineering, ethics, health, and politics.

Start that process yourself today by asking where the food you eat comes from.

EAT MORE FOOD

You eat food every day, right?

Not quite.

We can distinguish between food and food *products*. How do you know the difference? Food has no ingredients label!

Although the food industry has delivered massive benefits to the world's population by improving convenience and cost, a higher consumption of natural food, rather than human-made food, would no doubt result in greater health.

The weight loss and diet industry in particular has created a range of processed food products that do the exact opposite of what they advertise. The irony is that those foods labelled as the 'low-fat' or 'healthy' option have probably caused the biggest detriment to our collective health because they are manufactured with high salt, sugar, and other additives.

Eat less food products today and more food.

EAT LESS FOOD

"Eight parts of a full stomach sustain the man;
the other two sustain the doctor."

Old Japanese proverb

Overeating is easy to do.

In addition to the reasons we have covered so far this month, such as how fast we eat, studies have shown that we overeat when doing something else at the same time, such as watching TV or checking emails. Again, it's a lack of mindfulness—we are paying attention to something other than eating.

In Japan, they follow a culture of *Hara hachi bun me*, which roughly translates to "Eat until you are eight parts (out of ten) full", or "belly 80 percent full".

It isn't as hard as you may think. The stomach is about the size of your fist, though a little longer. It stretches of course, meaning you can fill a lot more in there. But it means we can often achieve satiety during the day by eating the amount of food that fits on the palm of your hand.

Try this today: stop eating before you are full and see how you feel.

EAT MORE PLANTS

So *what* should we eat?

Dr. David Katz, a nutrition expert and fellow of the Yale Center for Disease Prevention, looked at the main diets around the world in terms of beneficial health outcomes, comparing low carbohydrate, low fat, low glycemic, Mediterranean, mixed/balanced (DASH), Paleolithic, vegan, and elements of other diets.

He concluded that although there are positive features of several of them, no single one is best—if a diet is a set of rigid principles, health is not optimized. Rather, broader guidelines regarding what we eat that combine the best of each of the diets is ideal:

- A diet of minimally processed foods close to nature, predominantly plants, is decisively associated with health promotion and disease prevention.

Eating more plants is also one of the main things we can do to slow the planet's climate emergency—we simply can't sustain the world's increasing appetite for animal protein.

Veganism has experienced high growth in recent years. Whether you decide to pursue that route or not, just start eating more plants today. It is hugely beneficial for your health and that of the planet.

EAT MORE COLOURS

We've all heard it. Maintaining a 'balanced' diet has probably been the cornerstone of nutritional advice over the years. There are no 'bad' foods, it's the mix of what we consume that is key.

On one level, balance is required between carbohydrates, proteins, and fats, which are all necessary for the body to function properly.

Colours are another important element, and provide a useful roadmap—*if* those colours are natural.

Colourful fruits and vegetables contain *phytonutrients*, compounds that give plants their rich colours as well as their distinctive tastes and aromas. Phytonutrients also strengthen a plant's own immune system, protecting from threats in their natural environment such as disease and excessive sun. For humans, those same phytonutrients protect us from chronic diseases and have potent anti-cancer and anti-heart disease effects.

Filling a child's plate with all the colours of the rainbow might create some fun and encourage them to eat well. It could do the same for you! And don't forget that the skin often contains the highest concentration of phytonutrients, so take care peeling.

How many different colours can you eat today?

SWEET TOOTH?

ig Tobacco companies were the first type of businesses to come under intense public pressure that questioned their license to operate and forced them to pursue a path of transformation. 'Big Tech' companies are perhaps at the beginning of a similar trajectory. And 'Big Sugar' are currently in the thick of it.

Sugar is naturally present in many foods—it gives us a sustainable source of energy. The danger is in *added* sugar, which became an entire, and very powerful, industry. In the 1960s, the sugar industry actually paid scientists to play down the link between sugar and heart disease and instead promote saturated fat as the culprit.

Too much added sugar results in higher blood pressure, inflammation, weight gain, diabetes, and fatty liver disease, all of which are all linked to an increased risk for heart attack and stroke.

Life is to be lived. I'm the last person to say you mustn't enjoy dessert or a piece of chocolate. But, the simple fact remains: cutting down the amount of sugar you consume can save your life.

Start by *adding* less, or none at all.

INFLAMMATION IS EVERYTHING

You may have heard the word *inflammation* being used in terms of nutrition. Indeed, I've used it already this month. It is only as of late that I have found inflammation to be *the* most important thing in my life regarding my personal health. It's more important than sleep, exercise, and even nutrition in general terms.

Whether that's the same for you or not, it's worth getting to know how inflammation affects you. Global growth of auto-immune disease and other health disorders are a hint to me that it is critical for others too.

Inflammation is simply the body's response to harm. We need it as part of our immune response, such as swelling after twisting an ankle or a bruised limb after falling. It is useful, indeed critical, when it is a temporary response. Left unchecked however, inflammation becomes chronic. Obesity, stress, poor diet, lack of exercise and other lifestyle factors all contribute to chronic inflammation, which can then result in a range of diseases.

Inflammatory foods include foods that are fried, high in added sugar (cookies, doughnuts, and soft drinks), high in refined carbohydrates (white bread and white pasta), and red and processed meats.

Anti-inflammatory foods include colourful fruit and vegetables, extra virgin olive oil (unheated), turmeric, ginger, and omega-3 fats found in fish, nuts, and seeds.

Try eating less inflammatory and more anti-inflammatory foods today. Try it for the week and see how you feel.

A MOVEABLE FEAST

know the summer is here when a mass of huge, happy, bright watermelon is for sale. Then autumn arrives with piles of bright zesty tangerines. Seeing and eating these fruits is an important seasonal ritual which improves my mindfulness and overall well-being at each part of the year.

If you go to any market in Spain, you'll automatically know what time of year it is just by looking around at the colours and identifying the fruit and vegetables for sale—as well as their price and condition.

In many places however, we have created a world of convenience where we want—and can get—everything all year-round. But we pay a price for such convenience. Not only does food taste that much better when it's grown in its natural season, but it is cheaper to buy and also much better for the environment since it cuts down on transport.

What are the foods in peak season today? Try to keep your shopping to only those items and begin to enjoy the wax and wane of the seasons rather than suffer the tyranny of convenience.

BE LIKE WATER MY FRIEND

Ageing is viewed by many medical professionals as a drying-out process. So, good hydration is a key factor in maintaining optimum physical and mental health during all stages of life.

The body is 60% water and most studies show we need to drink between two and three litres every day.

If you find it difficult to drink that amount of water, the good news is that all drinks count—just watch the added sugar. Food counts too, especially fruits like those watermelon which are indeed mostly water.

Add in a consideration to *electrolytes,* they are helpful if you're suffering from more serious dehydration, for example after a very hard training session or when ill. You can create a homemade electrolyte drink by adding a good splash of pure fruit juice and a pinch of salt to a half litre of water. Give it a shake and you'll be surprised how similar it tastes to an expensive sports drink.

COFFEE?

I love coffee.

Everything about it—preparing it at home, all types of coffee machines, the culture of having a coffee outside the house, a *café con leche* somewhere in Spain or an espresso in Italy. And of course, I love drinking it.

It's good for you too.

Recent research from the UK suggests coffee reduces the risk of developing liver disease by almost one fifth and cuts deaths from chronic liver disease by nearly half. Having three to four cups per day was found to be most beneficial. Other studies have shown coffee to have a positive effect on cancer, heart disease, neurological health and depression.

Isn't it great when something you love is really good for you too?

OR TEA?

I love tea too.

Whereas coffee is a huge part of my day, tea is an important part of my evening. I find it incredibly refreshing, relaxing and *cleansing*. I seem to drink much more of it when I'm back home in the UK, where having a *cuppa* might be viewed as a similarly common part of the culture like an espresso in Italy. It contributes to our social wellbeing.

It's great for you too.

Numerous studies have found the powerful benefit of antioxidants found in tea which help to guard against cancer, heart disease and cognitive disease like Alzheimers. Green tea is frequently noted as the most beneficial and some studies even show it improves memory.

Isn't it great when something you love is really good for you too?

DECISIONS, DECISIONS, DECISIONS

How many decisions will you make today?

What to wear, what to eat for breakfast, how to travel to work, coffee or tea—the list goes on and that's before our day has hardly begun. How aware are you, though, of your energy or eating in regards to those decisions? How does the quality of your decisions change as your day progresses?

Decision fatigue refers to the deteriorating quality of decisions made by an individual after a long session of decision making. It can result in decision avoidance or simply the making of a bad decision.

For decades, the work of social psychologist Roy Baumeister linked decision fatigue to low glucose levels, and claimed that replenishing them restores the ability to make effective decisions.

This has been challenged as of late since Baumeister's original studies have not been replicated in other work. New research has stated that test subjects tend to follow a self-fulfilling prophecy. If we believe our capacity to make decisions is limited, then it will be.

Yet, bear in mind the simple facts. How we behave, and the decisions we make, will often be different if we are hungry, or having just had something to eat. And certain types of food which give us a sudden burst of energy may affect those decisions even more.

Witness any young child for evidence of that.

GI JOE

Pioneering work in elite sports at the University of Sydney enriched our understanding of the Glycemic Index (or GI) of foods and their effects.

The GI is a measure of the effects of carbohydrates on blood glucose levels. Carbohydrates that break down rapidly during digestion release glucose rapidly into the blood stream and have a high GI. Carbohydrates that break down slowly release glucose gradually into the bloodstream and have a low GI. All foods that have some carbohydrates are given a value in comparison to the reference of pure glucose, which has a value of 100.

Our brain recognizes the high GI foods and we make a bee-line for these when we feel tired or stressed. However, those positive effects quickly give way to feeling tired and hungry.

Spiking and crashing our blood sugar leads to excess insulin production which is then stored as fat. It can also result in craving a higher percentage of calories the next time we eat.

The irony here is that poor lifestyle choices are creating a Type 2 diabetes pandemic and this type of eating is very similar to the way that a diabetic must eat, strictly controlling blood sugar levels.

Take care especially with the GI of your breakfast. If you spike your blood sugar first thing in the morning, you're more likely to do it throughout the day.

GO FOR A GOOD GUT

Bacteria make up 13% of all biomass on earth. (To put that in perspective, all the mammals on earth make up only 5%). Every one of us has between 300 and 500 different species of bacteria in our gut. Sorry to be the one to tell you that.

We need to keep these bacteria happy. It's also important to promote good bacteria over bad. This is microbial health.

You do this through prebiotics and probiotics.

- *Prebiotics* feed your existing bacteria. They are found in the complex carbohydrates and fibre of foods like artichokes, asparagus, onions, garlic and apples.
- *Probiotics* are live bacteria. The good guys, of course. They mostly come in the form of probiotic supplements, but also exist in fermented foods like sauerkraut, kombucha, and kimchi.

It may not be the most appealing fact about our bodies, but taking care of gut health can make a huge difference to overall wellbeing.

WHERE'S THE PROTEIN?

The global food system will need to feed nine billion people or more by the year 2050.

The world's increasing appetite for animal protein will cause that system to break. One kilogram of beef requires 15,000 litres of water (around 2,000 gallons/pound) to produce—in the water required for the cow to drink, to grow feed and hay, and to keep stables and farmyards clean.

Studies have shown we can eat, sustainably, up to 100g (3.75 ounces) of meat per day. Beyond that, and the exponential rise of impacts results in an unsustainable future.

At present, 30% of the Earth's usable surface is covered by pasture land for animals, compared with just 4% of the surface used directly to feed humans. The total biomass of livestock is 60% of all mammals on earth—almost double that of the people on the planet and accounts for 5% of carbon dioxide emissions and 40% of methane emissions—a much more potent greenhouse gas. If the amount of meat we produce doubles, a likely scenario given current growing demand, livestock could be responsible for half as much climate impact as all of the world's cars, lorries, and airplanes.

Every single time you decide which protein to eat, it makes a difference.

ANYONE FOR CRICKETS?

nsect eating was common in many parts of Europe in the late 1800s.

Insects are a rich source of protein, fibre, and micronutrients such as iron and magnesium, as well as good fats, and are eaten in many parts of the world.

The World Food and Agriculture Organization of the United Nations makes the case that as the world's population grows, insects are key to future food security because they are far less carbon intensive than animals and need much less water. A range of entrepreneurs are springing up in an attempt to catch the wave and turn back attitudes to a former age. A few years ago, for example, I collaborated with Sens Foods, which makes sports protein bars from cricket flour. They taste great.

Not convinced?

Ok, maybe don't start with the crickets right away. How about Monday to Friday vegetarian, or pescatarian instead? Do you need to eat meat *every* day?

RE-DESIGN YOUR KITCHEN

Research has shown we're 30% more likely to eat the first thing we see.

Think about your own choices—especially at the end of a busy day when you're tired and hungry. I think we often find ourselves eating something just because it's the easy grab.

Research also shows that satisfying hunger depends on how full we perceive our plate to be. The conclusion to eat less and better manage weight? Use smaller plates!

The pandemic impelled many of us towards the therapeutic activity of gardening and it's likely we will need to be more self-sufficient in regards to food in the future. Even political upheaval such as Brexit in the UK have made people question reliable food supply. Can you grow some of your own food? You might be surprised at the boost of mental wellbeing that comes from growing a simple herb on your window sill.

How can you redesign your kitchen today to support better food consumption?

GOOD MOOD FOOD

D ifferent foods bring with them different moods.
Studies have found an association between depression and a diet rich in sugar-sweetened soft drinks, refined grains, and red meat. A Mediterranean diet, meanwhile, is rich in fruits, vegetables, olive oil, whole grains, and lean protein and lowers the risk of depression.

If you're in a good mood you're more likely to keep eating healthily to maintain that mood.

If you're in a bad mood, you go for foods you think will cheer you up, but end up re-enforcing that same negative motion.

It can be a hard cycle to break, but once you recognize it, it might be easier to try and break out of that bad mood. Eat the right food.

Go for good mood food. Follow the nudges of the past month.

FOOD WASTE

I n most of the developed world, food is cheap. Maybe too cheap. Americans spent one-fourth of their disposable income on food in the 1930s, dropping to one-fifth in the 1950s and one-tenth today. In Kenya and Pakistan today, people still spend up to one half of their income on food.

Food waste is a symptom of our modern age. Today, we produce about four billion metric tons of food per annum. Yet due to poor practices in harvesting, storage, and transportation, as well as market and consumer wastage, it is estimated that 30–50% (or 1.2–2 billion tons) of all food produced never reaches a human stomach. Some of these factors may be outside the range of us as consumers, but not all.

Don't take food for granted. Don't blindly follow the best-before, use-by, and sell-by dates which are merely indicators. Use your common sense instead. And try and use everything that you buy.

CELEBRATE LIFE

M illions of people around the world eat with chopsticks. Millions eat with their hands. What we eat and how we eat seems to be one of the biggest examples of what makes us different. Sometimes it seems we can't even agree on what is good for us to eat and what is bad.

Food is also one of the things that shows us how much we have in common and the one thing that brings us together.

We eat together at weddings and at funerals. We eat to herald the beginning of summer, the end of winter. We eat to celebrate something special in our lives. As a guest, we may be invited to share a meal. When we travel, we eat like the locals (or try to) and follow different customs and traditions.

To eat is to be human. It is a celebration of life. It nourishes the mind and the soul as much as the body.

NOTES ON YOUR JOURNEY THROUGH NUTRITION IN JUNE:

JULY

EXERCISE

THE SCHOOLRUN

When I was growing up, we didn't have a car. I had to walk or run to school every day. Then I'd run back home for lunch. And run back to school after lunch. Then run or walk home at the end of the day. I just Google mapped the distance from my childhood home to my school for the first time. It's around a mile (1.6km). That's four miles running and walking every day from the age of, I'm guessing, seven. Not quite the daily school odyssey that is sometimes reality in the developing world, but not too shabby either.

These days, for me, the 'school run' has a very different meaning. And I admit my part in adding to the problem in the city of Barcelona. There is huge traffic congestion at school drop-off and pick-up times, with many of the city's schools temporarily becoming illegal car parks.

This is a pattern reflected in many urban centres around the world. Our relationship today with movement in society has transformed and this change requires us to be more intentional with exercise. If we are, basically all aspects of our life will improve.

YOU HAVE A BODY

You have a body.

It's easy to forget. Until something goes wrong with it.

In many ways, this was the starting point for my own well-being journey because what I increasingly saw was busy executives living their lives from *the neck up*. I first got the idea after reading an article about the tennis player Roger Federer in *The New York Times*. The author commented on how gracefully Federer moved in a match. The expression of his physical self was the best example of what can be done and thus is a reminder to us all that we have a body.

As you go through your day today, gently remind yourself that you have a body. See what difference it makes to your behaviour.

MENS SANA IN CORPORE SANO

t's not a new idea, but the research that has come out in recent years that backs it is quite compelling.

Mens sana in corpore sano: the Latin phrase attributed to the Roman poet Juvenal from the early second century commonly translates to "a healthy mind in a healthy body".

Modern science supports its validity, with numerous studies showing the mental benefits of exercise. For example, neuroscience finds a 48-hour oxygen advantage to the brain after exercise, which specifically aids complex decision-making. Meanwhile, other research shows that exercise increases the size of the hippocampus, critical for memory, and therefore effectively aids in keeping ageing at bay.

Exercise provides value throughout our lives, not just as we get older. For example, studies have found that schoolchildren perform better on tests when they immediately follow a physical exercise class. And high levels of activity maintained through life also provide a *cognitive reserve* that act as a protective against dementia and other brain disorders in older people.

The first full line of Juvenal's poem is "you should pray for a healthy mind in a healthy body." Faith is important, indeed some things are outside our control, but you can do more than pray.

Commit to exercise.

PLATO WAS A CHAMPION WRESTLER

Going to the gym in Ancient Greece was considered a civic duty. The business of the day was done in the Agora. But people were too busy to do any actual thinking in the Agora. Sound familiar?

The thinking of the day was therefore done at the gym. Great philosophers including Aristotle and Socrates would give their lectures, ask the questions, push back the boundaries of human knowledge... and then wrestle!

The main Gymnasia of that time, the Lyceum and the Academy, were managed by Plato and Aristotle. Plato's *Lysis* describes an encounter that Socrates had when making his way from the Lyceum to the Academy, describing his main activity there, not as wrestling but "words, mostly words."

According to ancient texts, Plato was a champion wrestler, gaining honours at the Isthmian Games. This is where he got his name, in fact. *Platon* meaning broad in Greek. Originally called Aristocles after his grandfather, his wrestling coach is said to have called him Plato on account of his broad shoulders.

Think about when you do your best thinking. Exercise often plays a part.

THE GOLD FOR LITERATURE GOES TO...

The International Olympic Committee says that current president Thomas Bach is the first president in history who is also an Olympic Champion—Bach won Team Gold for West Germany in Foil Fencing in 1976.

Yet the very first President, the founder of the modern games, Pierre de Coubertin, won Gold for Literature in Stockholm in 1912. Writing under a pseudonym, his *Ode to Sport* poem allowed him to emulate the Ancient Greeks who had champions in sculpture, literature, and music in addition to the feats of strength and physical prowess.

De Coubertin, like the Greeks, wanted to promote a holistic form of human development through exercise. You can too.

OLYMPIC VALUES

Watching any Olympic Games, one is always struck anew by the immense physical power of these athletes. Yet their mental fortitude and virtue, while not physically visible, isn't far behind.

The Modern Games were founded on two main aims: to develop a more holistic form of education—with founder Pierre de Coubertin bemoaning the fact that education was overly specialised—and to promote peace between nations, with people around the world coming together in friendship and competition.

The concept of Olympism lasts to this day with the official Olympic values of excellence, friendship, and respect.

We can also develop different human virtues through exercise—discipline, courage, initiative, perseverance—but those can come later.

Start with those three Olympic values: excellence, friendship, and respect.

STRONGER, FASTER, SMARTER

The traditional Olympic motto is *Citius, Altius, Fortius* which is Latin for "faster, higher, stronger". Yet, given the brain benefits of exercise, perhaps Stronger, Faster, Smarter would be more appropriate.

As we age, the brain undergoes a process of remodelling known as neuroplasticity—it changes and reorganises in response to the environment, for example, during learning. When neuroplasticity is impaired different disorders, including Alzheimers, schizophrenia and depression, can result. Exercise is one of the most effective things we can do to boost neuroplasticity.

Numerous studies show that exercise improves attention, problem solving, processing speed, motor functioning, and memory. Part of the reason for this is that exercise produces a protein in the brain, BDNF (Brain-derived Neurotrophic Factor) which has been described by experts as 'Miracle-Gro' for the brain, and which fuels almost all the activities that lead to higher thought.

So, if you'd like to be smarter today, do some exercise.

LEGITIMACY

E xercise is often the first thing to get squeezed out. I get it. It happens to me too.

Time constraints for busy professionals were investigated by US management professor Russell Clayton in *Harvard Business Review*. He found that dedicating time to exercise, which some hard-working professionals may view as a luxury time item, is in fact even more valuable for those people with greater demands on their time. The reasoning is multiple—the structure and planning of training may be transferred with positive effect, improving self-efficacy, to other parts of a person's life, not to mention the more practical and readily acknowledged benefits of exercise, such as stress reduction. This is all so long as exercise doesn't translate into yet another thing to do, an item on an already long to-do list, and therefore an additional source of stress.

Legitimize physical training as a key part of a busy life that has benefits beyond the physical.

How will you build it in? Not just on occasion, but consistently?

THE MOST IMPORTANT THING

E ntrepreneurs are some of the busiest people in society. And the daily grind, without sufficient reset, results in many who have a poor level of health and wellbeing.

I remember reading a counterview in an article a few years ago in which an entrepreneur stated that exercise was the most important thing in her life. She acknowledged that this might sound strange to some because she was driving a fast-growth business forward at the same time as caring for family.

Yet her reasoning was simple.

If exercise didn't work, nothing else did. If she started to miss exercise sessions, little by little she would become less energised, less patient, less focused, making poorer food choices and worse decisions. Exercise was also for her—not the business or her family. And with exercise she could better take care of both.

With this logic, even though we all rightly value many other things, shouldn't exercise be the most important thing in your life too?

IT DOESN'T HAVE TO BE WORK

What type of exercise should you do?

The answer is different for each of us. Perhaps the exercise you choose can connect with your passion, or be shared with a friend, colleague, or family member. The key is that it doesn't become another source of stress or "work to do." With luck, you won't even be conscious that you are exercising— for instance, as in enjoying a dance class.

Beware of *slogging*, in which exercise becomes just another onerous task—sweaty, time consuming, and inefficient—and feelings of guilt arise because time is taken away from the workplace or home.

What exercise do you enjoy?

Don't make it another thing on your to-do list.

GYM HABITS

Gym memberships have sky-rocketed worldwide in the past few decades. And so have levels of obesity. Many of us are fitter on one level, but also fatter. There are different reasons for this of course, but let's consider a typical scenario to unpack the biggest factor:

Gym members drive there and back, drink a sports drink and have lunch. In most cases, this creates a calorie surplus rather than a deficit. The irony is that walking to and from the gym and *not* exercising may produce a bigger benefit.

The habits that surround the activity of going to the gym are therefore critical. For example, watch out that the physical tiredness from working hard at the gym may result in taking the escalator instead of the stairs or simply being more sedentary in general rather than walking in and around the house.

A hard gym session can also drain willpower. Studies show people are more likely to stop by Starbucks or McDonalds on the way home.

If you go to the gym today, fantastic. Just be careful what you do before and afterwards.

METS

Not the New York baseball version. I'm talking here about Metabolic Equivalent of Task.

The traditional science of exercise focused primarily on the need for time spent in higher intensity zones. For example, at least 20 minutes with the heart elevated to 70% of its maximum at least three times per week.

Newer advice is based on Metabolic Equivalent of Tasks, or MET, which considers the equivalent effort through higher or lower intensity. A MET is the amount of energy a person uses at rest. Two METs are two times the energy used, four METs are four times, and so on.

Recent guidelines advocate a minimum of 500 MET minutes/ week. Note, this doesn't mean 500 minutes of exercise. A high MET activity, such as fast running (greater than 15 km/h or 9 mph) is a 15 MET activity, which means just over a half-hour per week would achieve the minimum. Walking is in the 3–5 range, which would require 2.5 hours.

Research published in 2021 by an international team led by Glasgow Caledonian University looked at the ideal formula for health protection, based on a study of 130,000 people. They found three minutes of moderate to vigorous exercise per hour sitting, or 12 minutes of light exercise, to be the daily requirement for a longer life.

Find your own formula. Customise exercise to your own daily life.

THE HEART IS A MUSCLE

Your heart is the engine room for everything you do.

Every beat of that engine, which may be up to 100,000 times per day, comes in the form of a wave. Pumping 7,500 litres (2,000 gallons) of blood in a 24-hour period, tiny electrical currents drive the waves of movement that form the beating of your heart. A small electrical shock is first produced by pacemaker cells at the top of your heart. This electrical activity travels down through the muscle, contracting and passing on the current from cell to cell. After each has fired, it becomes momentarily unable to do so again, as if exhausted and needing a rest—until the next electrical shock from the pacemaker cells starts the whole process again.

We have 100,000 electrical shocks every day of our life, yet how often do we pay attention to it, or listen to it? Many adults are indeed frightened to consider it, and work it to its upper limit. Yet the heart is a muscle that needs to be maintained in good shape as like any other. It is a very useful barometer for our present state of health.

Take your pulse now and note in the space below. (Find your beat on your neck or wrist, fifteen seconds measurement, multiply by four).

Do this periodically and begin to understand what's going on. The following pages will help.

IN (AND OUT OF) THE ZONE

The most dangerous factor for health isn't that we take our heart rate to its maximum beat– rather that we exist in a perpetual middle or "grey zone" neither really working or truly resting that engine.

The generic formula for maximum heart rate is 220 beats per minute minus your age. This is just a starting point—some people may be higher, others lower. From here, we may consider heart zones. The use of a heart rate monitor will allow you to accurately gauge both your real maximum and your heart zones, yet you can very easily gauge your zones by considering perceived exertion, noted here:

50–60%	Relaxed, easy. Rhythmic breathing.
60–70%	Comfortable. Slightly deeper breathing, conversation possible.
70–80%	Moderate effort, more difficult to hold conversation.
80–90%	Hard effort and a bit uncomfortable. Breathing forceful.
90–100%	Unsustainable for a long period, laboured breathing.

Aim for exercise which covers all zones. Welcome training where you have the experience of having difficulty holding a conversation or breathing, at least for short periods.

TAKE A HIIT

T he slightly built Czech runner could be seen doing endless rounds of the track. He would pick up a stone on one side, run one lap fast, drop it off, rest for 30 seconds, and then do the same thing again. And again. Coaches would laugh at what they perceived as mindless repetition. But there was method in the madness. The year was 1944 and the runner's name was Emil Zatopek.

He went on to win the 5,000 meters, 10,000 meters, and the marathon at the 1952 Helsinki Olympics—a feat which has never been repeated. Zatopek's innovation of systematic interval training would transform track training, and eventually extend to other sports. Today, the same principle (known as High Intensity Interval Training, or HIIT) is used by people in their 80s to recover from heart-attacks.

Professor Martin Gibala and colleagues at McMaster University in Canada, a reference in HIIT training, settle on one minute as the optimum high-intensity period. Following such a protocol could give the following fifteen-minute interval session:

- 4-minute warm-up.
- 3 x 1-minute high intensity followed by 2-minute recovery.
- 4-minute cool down.

Adjusting intensity of effort may be conducted up and down a hill, on a bicycle, or by running fast and slow on a level piece of ground. Even combining walking and jogging. The key is to go beyond your comfort zone, recover and repeat.

Experiment with HIIT and reflect on how you feel.

THE 7-MINUTE WORKOUT

The 7-minute workout was designed by Chris Jordan, Director of Exercise Physiology at the Human Performance Institute in the US. Now owned by Johnson & Johnson, this is the same institute that gave rise to the Corporate Athlete methodology.

This particular workout is an example of HIIT training that also includes resistance training and encapsulates the science of METS (see entries of the past four days if you pick up *The Daily Reset* for the first time today!)

Twelve different exercises are followed for 30 seconds each, with 10 seconds rest between them, as follows:

1. Jumping jacks
2. Wall sit
3. Push-up
4. Abdominal crunch
5. Step-up onto chair
6. Squat
7. Triceps dip on chair
8. Plank
9. High knees running in place
10. Lunge
11. Push-up and rotation
12. Side plank

Countless free apps are available to guide you through this. The official Johnson & Johnson app is at: 7minuteworkout.jnj.com.

It's hard. But it's only seven minutes.

Give it a go.

PLEASED TO MEET YOU

E xercise is not just cardio. Overall health and fitness through exercise requires a healthy heart within a strong body. Resistance training has a variety of benefits including better posture, stronger bones, and joints that are more flexible. It's therefore of huge benefit to us as we age.

We begin to lose muscle mass in our early 30s and retention is a good marker of long-term health. Grip strength is one of the most accurate measures of predicting longevity and health at all ages. Numerous studies show the strong link between grip and mortality risk of all types, including cardiovascular disease.

Weight training is the typical means of doing resistance training and has huge benefits if done correctly. Consider also your own body weight—develop your core strength, stand more, try body weight exercises such as squats and planks.

Do what you can to keep that handshake strong.

DON'T DO IT ALONE

JogScotland is a Scottish Government sponsored initiative formed more than 20 years ago to encourage people to adopt a healthier lifestyle. There are almost 300 jog groups all over Scotland. I got a close-up view when I ran a sports tours company in Girona in the early 2000s and one of the Scottish groups came to Girona on a running holiday.

Having grown up in Scotland I know how a combination of lifestyle factors, including the weather, can result in a lack of physical activity and the resultant poor mental and physical health for people of all ages.

I was hugely impressed by what I saw when the running group visited, and I listened with interest to their experiences of joining the group. Deep friendships had been formed; lives transformed. They were a joy to be around and we remain in contact to this day.

The social matters. Greatly.

Don't (always) do it alone.

THE BEST TIME OF DAY (PART I)

When is the best time of day to exercise? It's a question I've been asked countless times over the years. Let's consider the work scenario first.

Getting up early is by far the most common strategy. Many people say that if they don't do it as soon as they get up, it simply won't happen. The principle disadvantage of course, despite any good intentions of adjusting bedtime, is getting less sleep. The good news is that physically fitter people need less sleep, with sleep cycles more efficient and physical movement during the day contributing to a higher percentage of stage four deep sleep at night.

A small minority of people do have the luxury of commuting to work, with cycling likely to be the most feasible option. Such working may be more pleasant than the typical commuter practice, though potentially stressful and dangerous depending on the roads available. Many people have maintained *faux commutes* on the bike even when working from home post-pandemic.

Exercise may also serve to help us—momentarily yet completely—forget about the trials at work or our personal life. Higher intensity in particular may allow one to get rid of the frustrations, stress, and rumination of the working day. At higher intensity, our body concentrates on essential biological functions and shuts down parts of the brain responsible for complex cognitive processing. In sum, we become a more primitive version of ourselves, which is useful to stop any over-thinking that causes stress.

Let me put forward a final suggestion: make exercise an integral part of your workday. Ask yourself the following question: how much quality work is accomplished in the mid-afternoon when our circadian rhythm dictates that we are at our lowest level of alertness?

Try different timeslots and see which fits you best.

THE BEST TIME OF DAY (PART II)

B ut really, you are probably still asking, when is the best time of day to exercise? Let's consider the performance scenario including specific objectives of exercise.

For physical and sports-related performance the answer is clear. We are physically stronger later in the day. Most athletics world records are broken in the afternoon or evening, when body temperature is highest, blood pressure is lowest, and lung function is more efficient.

For weight management, most studies settle on an early morning session when the body's hormonal set-up is best able to burn stored fat, especially on an empty stomach.

For mental performance, consider both the boost that exercise gives your brain as well as your peaks and valleys when you are naturally more alert. So, if you are naturally alert and perform well starting at 10am, exercise beforehand.

Take care, however, with excessive intensity because it can leave you tired and unable to think clearly. Watch out, also for exercising late at night because it can delay the time you fall asleep.

Again, try different timeslots and see which fits you best.

MAD DOGS AND SCOTSMEN

I love running in the extreme heat. In torrential rain too. Yet the puzzling thing for me when I came to live in Spain is that no-one goes outside to exercise when the weather isn't perfect.

I've encountered a similar attitude with people in different countries who will use weather as an excuse not to exercise, or at best, to remain indoors in (an often sterile) gymnasium.

For me, one of the best things about exercise is the connection with nature and all its elements. The experience reminds me that I'm alive and part of this wonderful planet.

Whatever the weather today (within reason of course!) get out there and enjoy the exercise.

CICADA RHYTHM

"You must learn to be still in the midst of
activity... and be vibrantly alive in repose."
Indira Gandhi

For me, one of the best parts of the Mediterranean summer is the sound of the cicada. These large insects are known for the courtship calls of males which are done by vibrating their hollow abdomen, or *tymbal*. Cicadas have been featured in literature since the time of Homer's *Iliad* and as motifs in art from the Chinese Shang dynasty. They have also been used in myth and folklore as symbols of carefree living and immortality.

When many cicadas are together, they produce an impressively loud sound. When I hear it, I know it's hot and its summer. I love running and hearing that sound.

For me, running is meditation. Finding stillness and presence in movement. Hearing the cicadas is part of that presence and stillness.

Through exercise, we can cultivate motion when still, and cultivate stillness when in motion.

44 SONGS

I rarely listen to music while running but understand it can have huge value.

I recently celebrated my 44th birthday and, as I've done on many of those days in previous years, I celebrated through exercise. I ran 44km, a kilometre for every year of my life, fuelled by 44 special songs.

I wasn't in great shape and probably wouldn't have finished if not for the songs. Flagging at different points on the *Carretera de les Aigües* overlooking Barcelona, a song would start which immediately transported me to another time, another place, a joyful moment in my life. Sometimes it was nothing specific, just a warm feeling.

That run on my birthday was a hugely emotional, almost spiritual, experience based on the physical exercise.

How can you combine all three?

WHAT IT FEELS LIKE TO BE AN OLYMPIAN

I f you watched any of the 2020 Tokyo Olympics you may have marvelled at the superhuman feats of the athletes. Yet, for me, these latest Games were the first time I noticed a transparency and vulnerability around what it takes to produce those performances, particularly around the topic of mental health. There was a pulling back of the curtain, let's say.

It reminded me of an interview the English distance runner Brendan Foster gave some years ago A reporter asked about *what it feels like to be an Olympian?* Foster replied: *I'm just tired, tired all the time.*

You may not be training for the Olympics, but bear in mind that exercise, like anything in life, isn't good for you when taken to the extreme. Even Plato commented on athletes who ignored balance—that they became unadaptable and sluggish and need too much sleep. He said the ultimate goal was to bring the body and mind "into tune with one another by adjusting the tension of each to the right pitch."

Consider your own 'pitch' as you develop exercise as a key element in your life.

RE-FUEL

At the 2008 Beijing Olympics, as Michael Phelps chased eight swimming golds, many newspapers around the world picked up on a story that he was consuming 12,000 calories per day, with accompanying photos to show what that looked like in terms of food. In case you're wondering, it's a lot.

The story was greatly exaggerated—he later clarified he ate nowhere near 12,000 calories per day. Yet the story highlights the huge importance of the necessary input (or fuel) for desired outputs.

Of the many benefits of exercise is the closer relationship with what we eat and drink. As a young athlete, I could eat pretty much anything—it all burned up in my daily training and racing. Now I need to be much more mindful of what I eat and how that connects with exercise, before and after.

One thing to consider is how to refuel after exercise, preferably in the 30–40 minutes afterwards. This is when special enzymes are released which optimize absorption of the vitamins and minerals needed to recover.

SNACKING IS GOOD FOR YOU

How much time will you have available for exercise today? The answer for most of us is not a lot.

But that doesn't matter.

'Exercise snacking' or micro-workouts is a way of looking at exercise that combines short duration with repetition throughout the day. Even the busiest amongst us has those small pockets of time to do something.

Without being too intentional, I've built up my own exercise snacks over the years. I do squats in the shower, lift kettlebells in the time my coffee machine takes to make a double espresso, and I do press-ups before going to bed. This can all be measured in seconds and takes nothing from the normal flow of my day, but added together it makes for a significant weekly exercise regime. I haven't been to a strength conditioning class for years and I don't think I need to.

What 'snacks' can you build in?

HAVE AN OBJECTIVE

At the start of every academic year when I was a University student I would sit down with my wonderful coach Anne-Marie Hughes and plan the cross-country season. The big goal would get marked down first—the Scottish University Championships—followed by other key races and finally the training plan that would ensure I had the best chance of performing well at those races.

In the depths of a Scottish winter, that plan gave me the necessary focus and rationale when I questioned why I was running around an empty park in torrential rain.

I rarely race nowadays but having an objective and the wider planning that goes with it is still invaluable. It saves me from just drifting along. It also keeps me safe. Periodisation is the athletic principle whereby we increase load over a number of weeks, improving performance, and then decrease or *taper* before injury or illness can take hold.

So, do you need to go harder today? Further? Or maybe it's time to take it down a notch. Don't just grind away every day.

What's the objective?

IT'S A MARATHON, NOT A SPRINT

The marathon is considered the ultimate running experience but I never truly understood until I experienced it myself. There are four things I've learned that I believe can be applied to life too.

Keep calm when things aren't going well
In the marathon, no matter how well prepared you are, you will always have that 'bad patch'. The key is not to panic, assess why it is happening and action accordingly. Is it a physical injury? Is it fuel-related? Is it simply mental? Life too. Here's the key thing— that bad patch will pass. As Charles Swindoll remarked, "10% of life is what happens to you, the other 90% is how you react to it."

A good spell will come, be ready
As a flip side to the above there will be times when you have 'good legs'. Such energy may come from the crowd or food you eat. It could be a following wind or downhill stretch of the course. In both a marathon and my daily life I am attentive to these good moments. Just as important is that I always believe there to be a good moment to come.

Fuel consistently
Drinking and eating while running at pace isn't easy to do, but it is essential for the marathon. The energy you take in at an early stage of the race is used later. Many of us go through life too at a fast pace, so much so that we forget about taking that energy in.

continued to next page

continued from previous page

Construct your own reality

What's the big thing you hear from friends who have run the marathon? *Watch out for hitting the wall! You're dead at 30km!* The science supports this but I would guess the majority of who suffer are accepting other people's reality. It is a self-fulfilling prophecy. Break through the wall. Always question the 'facts'. Find your own truth in different parts of your life.

WHO'S YOUR COACH?

The best athletes in the world, legends of any sport, need a coach. Not because the coach is (or was) better, but for the value of having someone look in from the outside. A young athlete may benefit from the technical knowledge that a coach can impart, but as they advance through their career this becomes less important. It then becomes about someone always looking out for your best interests—a gentle word here, a guiding hand there, a rollicking if required.

I think we can all benefit from that. Whether you use exercise for better athletic performance, improved health, or simply relaxation, consider a coach—formal or not.

Who could be that coach for you?

JULY 30

FINDING FLOW

I n his seminal work, Mihály Csíkszentmihályi identified sport as one of the main fields where high performance and effortlessness combined to create the flow state.

Exercise can be hard. It can be tiring. Sometimes we don't want to do it.

But sometimes everything clicks into place. Not only are we the best we can be (faster, higher, stronger, more coordinated, whatever your exercise is) but it's also so *easy*. It's as if we're observers of what we're doing—ever so slightly detached—rather than being the agent of that action.

When it happens, it's special. But it doesn't tend to last long.

Embrace it. Appreciate it.

And if you've yet to experience it, you will. Just keep searching.

ME TIME

t's time for you.

If you want to make exercise social, or targeted towards better performance, fantastic. Equally, it can be your own meditation. You get to decide.

You are the owner of this time. Exercise, ultimately, is the means by which you can build a relationship between your body and your mind.

Physical health and mental health together. Now that's something worth aiming for.

AUGUST

PURPOSE

TIME TO REFLECT

[MY JOURNAL]

Whether you're on the beach or in the mountains, or simply enjoying the summer months and a temporary lull from normal working life, August is a good month to reflect.

In Spain, where I have lived now for nearly 20 years, August is traditionally the month when things simply stop. Although this trend has lessened slightly in the past several years, it has long been a cultural hallmark of most of Southern Europe.

I reflected deeply on this phenomenon this past August. I was in the final drafts of *The Daily Reset* and, in between long writing stretches, I would walk my dog around the deserted streets of Barcelona. It felt like both the city and I were burrowing into ourselves, regenerating and preparing to burst into the hive of activity that comes with Autumn routines.

Don't stop this month. Rest, absolutely. But think, deeply.

Reflect on purpose.

[YOUR JOURNAL]

ARE YOU WELL?

A simple question. Three words. Yet one of the biggest changes I noticed during the pandemic was "well" replacing the previous stalwart of opening small talk, "busy".

We asked this of our friends, families, colleagues, clients—and in the midst of the irony that has been increased social contact at greater social distance—new acquaintances from different spheres of our lives, and friends we haven't spoken to in years.

In work relationships, we have been made acutely aware of any particular vulnerabilities of colleagues' working from home situation, and 'checking-in without checking-up' may even have helped us to build closer relationships and stronger teams.

Ask someone today—and listen to the answer.

Just as important, ask yourself.

ASKING THE RIGHT QUESTIONS

The daily reset is about reform. Reform of the way we think, of the way we do and see things. Reform of the questions we ask. Here are six questions to consider at the start of this month:

1. What are the uniquely good things that happened to me during the pandemic, for which I was grateful, and which I want to retain moving forward?

2. What are the things that are most causing me worry and stress? How do I remember that I shouldn't spend too much energy on things outside my control?

3. How do I maintain self-care as a primary concern, and the means of best taking care of my family and colleagues?

4. How might I create meaning in the work I do each day, and connect that to a positive impact on society?

5. How do I best connect with others on a daily basis?

6. How do I best connect with myself on a daily basis?

THE GREATEST QUESTION IN HISTORY

What is a good life?

It's a question many have asked during the shared global trauma of the pandemic. It led to many people describing the great reset and, later, as some decided life was too short to be miserable at work, the great resignation.

It's also a question asked by some of history's greatest philosophers. Aristotle talked of the importance of fulfilment, learning and virtue. Confucius highlighted rituals and *tao* which can be roughly translated to path, as in finding our own path.

More recent academic instruments focus on elements such as interest in ones' own life, respect from others, quality of relationships, ability to meet monthly living expenses, and, of course, whether we understand our purpose.

There are many factors to consider, which reflects the richness of life. I'll leave you with one thought to consider today, from the work of American psychologist and academic Ed Diener:

I am a good person and live a good life.

DIAMONDS ARE FOREVER

I n 1971, in his last official outing as James Bond in "Diamonds Are Forever", Sir Sean Connery gave every penny of his 1.2 million dollar salary to set up the Scottish International Education Trust, which supports exceptional young Scottish talent, in any field, in need of financial assistance.

In the year 2001, the trust supported my Doctoral research tour of North America, including a semester at Stanford that continues to add value to my career today. Thanks to the former James Bond, a young boy from Motherwell got to travel the world and begin to believe in what was possible.

Thank you, Sean.

RIPPLES IN THE WATER

I knocked on a lot of doors growing up. And a lot of them opened. I went to an excellent University just 20 miles from my home, worked through placements at several leading organisations and received a good amount of financial support to travel the world and continue my learning journey.

I was always proactive, yes, but I was also fortunate to find many people willing to open the door. It's made me determined to find ways to positively impact the health and wellbeing of as many people as possible. This is my purpose.

I'm also more attuned to how I can open doors for others. Most people would flourish if they were given the opportunity. In a world of increasing inequality, how can we all play a part in ensuring a fair system? How can we make sure we don't operate an increasingly closed or fixed game?

We all have an opportunity, each day, to leave our own legacy through our actions and words, and through the actions of words of the people we lift up.

How can you let down the ladder to someone today?

THANK YOU CLAN SIMPSON

I first met Rory Simpson the same year he started as the Chief Learning Officer of Telefónica in 2011. From the first encounter he was open, curious to know more about me, and supportive.

Many of the entries this month are inspired not only by Rory, who is an expert in the area of purpose, but also by his family. Both his mother Myrtle and father Hugh were polar explorers and each recipients of the Polar Medal, an honour that has been awarded to members of both Captain Scott's and Ernest Shackleton's expeditions of the early 20ᵗʰ Century. Rory's brothers and sisters, Bruce, Robin, and Rona are similarly high-achieving, warm, and generous, and act as if your success is integral to their own happiness.

Thank you to all of the Simpson family.

Who cheers the loudest for you when you are winning? Or does everything in their power to ensure you do?

THE SEARCH IS THE REWARD

"He who has a why to live can bear almost
any how."

Friedrich Nietzsche

Have you found your purpose in life?
This is where your talent meets impact and passion to
create something truly unique—where you feel aligned,
whole, and on the right path.

Don't worry if this doesn't reveal itself easily. For many, it
doesn't. Take your time and build towards it. Explore, experiment,
find out new things about yourself.

Academic research shows that an individual's sense of purpose
isn't fixed but changes over our life. Kendall Bronk, a Professor
of Psychology at Claremont Graduate University, says in a 2009
paper which looked at purpose in three different age-groups that
it "is a project that endures across the lifespan." It can be clarified,
strengthened, and, for some, serve as a lifelong aspiration, or a
guiding star.

The search itself can be the reward.

IKIGAI

*I*kigai is a Japanese word that loosely translates to "a reason for being." It is the sweet spot of purpose and impact that leads to true wellbeing. It also considers practicality and feasibility. For most people, chasing dreams and following our passion is all well and good but what if you can't pay the rent or mortgage while you do so? *Ikigai* is therefore a combination of the following aspects:

- What do you love?
- What are you good at?
- What does the world need?
- What can you be paid to do?

These combine to give the passion, profession, mission, and vocation that delivers the higher gift of *Ikigai*. How can you use them to guide your search for purpose?

Beware another Japanese term, *Karoshi*, which translates to "death by overwork". You make the choice.

YOUR LIFE'S WORK

All life is not work.

But, for most of us, work is a significant part of life and the two cannot be separated. Work is often a source of purpose since it offers an opportunity to have an impact—but this can go too far, causing imbalance and a lack of alignment with non-working life.

Considering the other extreme, can you pursue your search for purpose and forget about work completely? Perhaps. Though your wellbeing—just as when work takes over completely—mustn't be forgotten along with it.

Many figures in history have changed the world, yet been unhappy. Was this fulfilling their purpose? If so, it is a shame that they had to sacrifice their one life to do so.

As you search for purpose, don't forget about wellbeing. Remember, *if you're not well at work, you're not well at home, and if you're not well at home, you're not well at work.*

If we are lucky, wellbeing might just be the means by which we can find, and amplify, our purpose.

MEANING AT WORK

The COVID-19 pandemic made millions around the world question what they were doing every day, and ask whether their jobs helped them pursue their purpose. The companies I saw who were best at riding out the early storm were able to help people grasp the impact of their daily efforts. Employees were able to put a face to the people they were helping in a time of great need and thus felt the positive impact of their actions.

McKinsey reports that people who live their purpose at work are more productive than people who don't. They are also healthier, more resilient, and more likely to stay at the company—and if they feel the company doesn't provide the means for them to live their purpose at work and find meaning, they will leave for one that does.

McKinsey offers three types of purpose for an individual: purpose from the organization directly, purpose from work activities, and purpose outside of work. Based on this, ask yourself the following three questions:

- Do you feel aligned with the purpose and culture of your company?
- Are you energized and do you find meaning in the work you do each day?
- Are you able to pursue your purpose and interests outside of work, whether for yourself, family, or community?

DESERT ISLAND DISCS

*D*esert Island Discs is a radio programme broadcast by the BBC since the 1940s and is one of the world's longest-running radio shows. Each week a guest, called a 'castaway', is asked to choose eight recordings (usually, but not always, music), a book and a luxury item they would take if they were to be castaway on a desert island, and then discuss their lives and the reasons for their choices. Guests invariably come to the show thinking it will be easy but they often leave crying. Such is the emotion unleashed through hidden memories.

Think about your own Desert Island Discs. Eight songs that represent your life so far. Begin with your young life as a child, maybe it's your earliest memories of music. Next, think about your teens, often a hugely important time for one's relationship with music, identity and companionship. Moving on then to young adulthood, relationships, family, special moments, perhaps even difficult moments through which you made it to the other side.

What are these eight songs?

From personal experience, I can tell you this exercise is a time-machine. It is a hugely powerful, visceral encounter with yourself that unleashes deep-lying memories and emotions. Be prepared.

THE GOLDEN GATE BRIDGE

"Do one thing every day that scares you."
Eleanor Roosevelt

n 2001, when I was a visiting researcher at Stanford, my girlfriend (now wife) Pamela came to visit from London. We took a weekend trip to San Francisco which included a boat ride to Sausalito. The plan was to have lunch there and walk back over the Golden Gate Bridge.

We had a great day until I discovered, halfway across the bridge, that I had vertigo. I had never previously thought heights to be an issue, but there I was, close to freezing on the spot in a panic-induced long walk across the rest of the bridge. It was terrifying.

It made me question my fears, subsequently tracing part of the problem to a childhood accident. I then pushed up against them, mostly through high mountain passes on my road bike over the years.

When was the last time you did something that filled you with fear?

Fear can tell us a lot about ourselves, about where we came from and where we're going. Yet it's a place we don't go to. We tend to stick within our comfort zone, especially as we age.

Do you know your fears?

Get a little closer and see what happens.

ZONES OF DISCOMFORT

"One can choose to go back toward safety or forward toward growth. Growth must be chosen again and again; fear must be overcome again and again."

Abraham Maslow

The pandemic was a brutal experience for millions around the world. Yet it also forced people to change for the better. The 'comfort to growth zone' model from the positive psychology field may accurately describe the journey for many:

Comfort Zone
Here we feel safe and secure, but static. No risk but no growth either.

Fear Zone
On first leaving the comfort zone, you may lack self-confidence. You're easily affected by the criticism of others and look for excuses.

Learning Zone
Next comes the learning zone where you're better able to deal with challenges and acquire new skills that help you progress.

Growth Zone
Ultimately, you're in the growth phase where you're able to reflect on dreams, aspiration, and purpose as well as do what you need to do in the moment.

Which zone do you occupy in the various parts of your life? Ask yourself if you need to set forth and embrace some fear.

MAKE TIME FOR LEARNING

We're living longer lives. At the same time, the increasing pace of change in the world means that many things we do learn become obsolete much faster than they did in the past.

This changes the classic model of education whereby we have an intense learning block in our youth (school and university) that we then apply through the rest of our lives.

Being more intentional with learning is therefore a necessity. Create space for it. Put it in the diary. Don't be afraid of poor performance or failure when trying new things because this is also a valuable part of the process.

McKinsey suggests the 3 x 3 x 3 method to help be more intentional with learning. The first 3 corresponds to the number of development goals. They advise a single goal as being insufficient but not to be laden with too many either. The second 3 is the duration—three months as an initial plan before checking in on how the learning is going and whether to re-calibrate. The third 3 is involving three other people to help you in the learning journey.

Will 3 x 3 x 3 work for you?

RECONNECTING

I n June 2016, I raced track for the first time in over a decade. At 39 years of age, I had more than two decades on most of my fellow competitors lining up for the 5,000m Barcelona athletics league meet. I made a decent fist of it, forcing the pace midway and stretching the pack before three younger and faster athletes kicked away in the closing laps.

I was ecstatic. I didn't care so much about the result but was fully absorbed in the experience—the energy of youth buzzing around the track on the warmup, the nervousness at the call to the start, the dry mouth as we toed the line and awaited the gun, the sun setting as we rounded the last lap, the tired legs that signalled accomplishment, and the camaraderie of the infield warm-down. All of it reconnected me to my former self. And it was wonderful.

How can you reconnect to your former self?

DO YOU REMEMBER
THE FIRST TIME?

was vaguely aware, when I sat down, of the others in my row. But as we neared the end of the taxi and were in queue for take-off, I began to pay closer attention to the young brother and sister glued to the window and talking excitedly to their mother. They hushed as we monetarily paused and then squealed with delight as we hurtled along the tarmac. Their enthusiasm was contagious. I found myself being swept along in their joy as we became airborne. It was the first time (as I enquired a few minutes later to their mother) that these young children had left the surface of the earth.

Studies show that the more people fly, the more likely they are to take the aisle seat. *The Economist* commented that the window seat is for dreamers and the aisle seat for cynics.

Our lives are often caught in a never-ending quest for convenience and optimisation. But, maybe, we should put that to one side now and again and fill ourselves with the childlike wonder of accelerating 0–180mph in ten seconds, propelling 300 metric tons of engineered marvel into the air before cruising at 37,000 feet and over 500mph. No matter how many times you've done it, I challenge you to try and capture the thrill of that first-time experience. It may come easier than you might expect.

When was the last time you did something for the first time?

Take the window seat.

MISREMEMBERING

D o you remember where you were when the airplanes hit the World Trade Center in New York on 11th September 2001? (There's a chance you weren't born, or were far too young to hold a memory but please stick with me!)

I was in Pittsburgh, studying at Carnegie Mellon University. We set up a television in the research centre office and watched aghast as the events unfolded. That night I went to a large hotel for an academic conference and remember people outside with placards demanding justice. I vividly recall George W. Bush's televised address that night and the frantic calls from my family in Scotland to check that I was ok.

Lots of detail. Vivid memories. Memories we can trust right? Not quite.

Researchers in the US looked at how memories of personal experience shift with time, based on the 9/11 attacks. In the days that followed they asked people about their experience; where they were, who they were with and how they reacted to the news. They were questioned again after a one-year, three-year and ten-year interval. More than 40% of the respondents markedly changed their recollections of the event with time. Curiously, the stories underwent the greatest change at the one year mark, after which point they tended to tell the same false story in the decade that followed.

Our memory plays tricks on us. Don't base everything on what you think happened in the past.

Find the path forward without being restricted by where you think you came from.

THE NUMBER ONE PERSON IN YOUR LIFE

Have you read Jordan Peterson's *12 Rules for Life*? Rule number two is 'Treat yourself like someone you are responsible for helping.' As Peterson details, we often take care of others, even pets, better than we take care of ourselves.

This month focuses a lot on our relationship with ourselves. Self-respect is an important starting point.

Be kind… to yourself. Consider your daily thoughts and actions. If you were to direct them at cherished person in your life, how would you feel?

SELF TALK

Time helps heal all wounds.

We can be good at offering advice and insight to others and not so good at applying that same advice to ourselves.

Both concepts contain some element of *distance*—distance from ourselves and our situation. In stressful or pressurised times, we tend to zoom in on issues, making them worse. Zooming out helps us gain perspective and informs our better judgement.

Various studies show that talking to ourselves, internally, in the third person (for example, I might say to myself during a tough task, *you can do this Steven!*) can create a degree of psychological distance that helps control negative emotions, and also improve performance and wisdom. In times of high stress, we may begin to think of ourselves in a fashion more similar to how we think of others, which helps clear any emotional fog and overcome personal bias.

In a busy daily life checking in with yourself is key. We maintain a dialogue with important people in our life—remember to do the same with yourself. Just be careful with the intense self-talk and getting too close.

Try talking to yourself in the third person to maintain distance and perspective.

SELF-CARE IS NOT SELFISH

For many years, I've done an exercise with my workshop participants whereby they take a piece of paper and map out their typical day. The full 24 hours. Maybe you can try it in the space below.

It's amazing how we can live reality day-in, day-out, for years, but only fully understand what is happening when it is down on paper in front of us. The most common insight that people have from this exercise is: 'I don't have any time for me!'

From waking to sleeping, nearly every moment is for others: family, friends, work. Yet, how do you ensure that all these other areas of your life get the best you? By taking care of *you*. Take time for yourself, invest in your passions and hobbies, spend time alone. Block it as if it was a key meeting in your calendar, set notifications, write post-it reminders. Whatever works.

Self-care is not selfish.

WHAT ARE YOUR VALUES?

We're often aware of the values of our company, but what about our own values? Your values define your behaviour, like an operating manual, and tell you how to act within a given context. They are a strong anchor.

Thinking on who or what inspires you can lead you towards your personal values. Thinking about what drives you crazy also helps! It's in these instances that you'll likely find your own values being infringed, so having an 'anti-role model' can be useful.

What are some examples of values? Fairness perhaps, loyalty, trust, authenticity, love. There is no shortage of values out there but what are the small subset you hold most dear? Reflect on the following questions that Rory Simpson has used at Universitas Telefónica over the years to help guide thousands of people in the next stage of their lives:

- Who are your heroes?
  What qualities do they possess?
- Recall a time in your life when you made a stand on an important issue. What values were you "protecting" at that time?
- What is your favourite poem, book, or movie?
- What would you be prepared to die for? If it's an idea, person, or possession, ask yourself what value(s) they represent.

Take some time to write down the values that best represent you, your beliefs, and behaviour. My recommendation would be to try and define at least three and perhaps a maximum of five.

FIND YOUR MORAL COMPASS

I spent some time with my young son recently in the wonderful turquoise seas off Formentera, Spain. We were having fun and I was also trying to encourage him to be mindful of where he was as a means of being more independent and safer in open water.

I asked him to look at his mother every few minutes sitting on the beach. Given the underlying currents, we moved significantly from our original spot in a short space of time, surprising even me.

From time to time, we all experience similar *drifts*. Without noticing it, we may suddenly find ourselves far away from who we really are and the things that keep us centred. This is why the daily reset is so important.

How to combat personal drift? By defining your moral compass, or North Star—many of the questions we have asked so far this month address this.

Your moral compass will help you navigate through both calm and rough seas—even when the underlying currents are strong and you can't see the way through the fog.

PIVOTS AND PURPOSE

*P*ivot was a commonly used word during the initial stages of
the pandemic.

Organisations that were slow to adopt change for years
suddenly implemented all manner of new innovations. The pivot
allowed them to survive the crisis, but many are now finding long-
term value in these innovations, which will allow them to thrive
in the post-pandemic world.

The early stages of the pandemic also forced many organisations to reflect on why they exist. The hotel industry, being one of
the hardest hit sectors, was no exception. Hilton had no choice but
to shut many of its hotels, but at the same time the company gave
millions of free rooms to healthcare workers. They doubled down
on their mission and purpose of hospitality and care, providing a
safe space for travellers.

I spoke to the Managing Director of Hilton in the UK and
Ireland, Stephen Cassidy, during 2020 and he told me how moti-
vated staff became from providing a valuable service to NHS staff.
Furthermore, they came up with new ways of safely serving these
people, which now continues to add value to the traditional hotel
service.

It takes bravery to change, to affect an about-face. Purpose
gives you that confidence.

THE POWER OF WHY

How great leaders inspire action by Simon Sinek is one of the most watched TED talks with (at the time of this writing) more than 55 million views.

Sinek insists on the importance of purpose. He talks of an individual's purpose, but also that of the team and company. He says consumers don't buy what you do, they buy *why* you do it.

One example he gives is that of the Wright brothers and their purpose to achieve powered human flight. They competed with Samuel Pierpont Langley, who had all the budget, knowledge, and advice from the greatest consultants of the day but lacked real purpose other than his desire for fame. The Wright brothers did it, of course, taking off on the 17th of December 1903, and the aircraft industry was born. Purpose got them through countless setbacks, accidents, and economic challenges. They had a constant belief that they could achieve it. A dream. And they knew why they were doing it.

You probably know what you are doing (or have done) today. But *why* are you doing it?

LA SAGRADA FAMÍLIA

Each morning the slightly dishevelled 73 year-old would wake in his small workshop basement and get to work, just as he had for the past 43 years. He had a purpose that drove his daily work, here and elsewhere, for most of his life. His name was Antoni Gaudí and he was working on the Sagrada Família.

Gaudí's strong purpose was to celebrate the work of God by creating architectural forms derived from God's work: nature. He is the creator of many of the Barcelona's most famous buildings, parks, street lamps, and benches. And while he accepted the contracts of the rich families and merchants of the city as a means of funding his one true purpose, he lived humbly—so much so that when he died, hit by a tram on the way to attend mass, people thought he was a beggar.

Gaudí said "nothing is art if it does not come from nature," and had a vision, not just of buildings, but also of whole cities and modern living industrial ecosystems that were part of nature.

To this day, the truly awe-inspiring structure of the Sagrada Família rises into the sky and will keep gaining height until its completion scheduled for the year 2026, 100 years after Gaudí's death.

To view it from the outside is one thing. To go inside is to witness an other-worldly beauty. I don't think I'm alone in saying I cried when I did so. That is the power of purpose.

THE GREAT RESIGNATION

Darling, you got to let me know
Should I stay or should I go?
If you say that you are mine
I'll be here until the end of time
So you got to let me know
Should I stay or should I go?
Should I Stay or Should I Go, The Clash
Lyrics by Joe Strummer and Mick Jones

The summer of 2021 gave rise to *The Great Resignation*. A Microsoft survey of 30,000 global workers showed more than 40% were considering quitting or changing professions. Department of Labor statistics in the US showed four million people quitting their jobs in April 2021, the biggest spike on record.

If you're thinking of making a change, you're not alone. Priorities are shifting. People are waking up. Being brave.

But so too are organisations. I have hope that the reasons people feel they need to leave their jobs will soon be addressed as employers change their own ways of doing things.

Whatever you decide, use the tools and questions this month to make the right decision for you.

THE GUARDIAN
OF THE MOUNTAIN

A couple of years ago, to celebrate the approaching Christmas and New Year season, my Catalan trail running buddies and I set off on a special run in the nearby Montseny mountains. We usually run together between one and two hours on the weekends in the natural Parc Collserola, which borders the city of Barcelona and peaks around 500m above sea level. Montseny rises over 1700m and a six-hour trail run was in prospect, including two of the big climbs.

I was nervous.

But I shouldn't have been.

At the beginning of the first main climb of the day, a dog appeared from nowhere. We thought he was with some other runners or hikers, but he was alone. He would run alongside us for several minutes, disappear, then come back. Sometimes he would come back quickly. Sometimes an hour would pass. He stayed with us until our final ascent of the day. I looked at the name tag hanging around his neck—*Montseny* (the name of the mountain). I think he spends his days guiding people up the climbs. A true spirit of the mountain.

I believe we all have a guardian. We may feel loneliness at different times of our lives but I'd like to think there is always someone, or something, watching out for us. Every one of us. Maybe you just need to look around you.

CARPE DIEM

I n June 2021, I noticed some swelling in my neck glands. A common occurrence as a child, I didn't think too much about it until a few weeks had passed and the swelling remained. An initial Ear-Nose-Throat consultation dismissed it as of no importance.

Then one day the swelling got *really* big and off to the emergency room I went. I soon found myself undergoing a cranial MRI for the possible presence of a tumour.

The odds were in my favour of course. The lesser possibility was a tumour, which even if found would likely be benign. But I still had a worrisome, and deeply reflective, five days before the results were confirmed.

I committed to several new intentions over those five days, including this book, which was finally sparked into action after it had been envisioned for the preceding several months.

I'm fit and healthy. I do what I can to keep illness and disease at bay. But I'm now entering middle age. There's no guarantee.

Each day counts. That's enough purpose for starters.

DRAW YOUR LIFELINE

Try and find an hour today when you won't be disturbed. In the middle of a sheet of paper (or below if you feel there is space) draw a horizontal line that represents your life from birth to the present day. Next, draw a line vertically with high points at the top and low points at the bottom. Now reflect and note these highs and lows, the good and the bad. Join all events by tracing a line.

How do you feel?

ENJOY THE RIDE

I f things aren't going well right now, it will pass.
If you're on top of the world, it will also pass.
That is the richness of life. And I'm sure this month of August, like any other this year, has had its ups and downs.

Whether you have found your purpose, or you're still searching, the most important thing is to enjoy the ride.

NOTES ON YOUR JOURNEY THROUGH PURPOSE IN AUGUST:

SEPTEMBER

WAYS OF WORKING

A NEW YEAR

I n many ways, I consider September to be the first month of the year. Maybe it's my academic background, eagerly expecting the start of University life at this time each year. The feeling was only compounded by my life in Spain, coming off the back of a sleepy month of August when most of the professional class would return from the beach and mountain to restart their normal routine.

The beginning of a new year is often filled with intention and aspiration. We look ahead to bold new objectives and ambitious plans. Maybe there's anxiety and nervousness around a sense of not being quite ready to return.

Whatever your state of mind, let's get back to work.

And think most of all on the manner in which you do that work.

THE FIRST 15 MINUTES

Y ou woke up today. You got out of bed. And then?

The bathroom perhaps. The coffee machine. Your phone.

If *The Daily Reset* makes it as part of those opening morning rituals, just as *The Daily Stoic* does in my own day, I'm truly humbled.

What I'm trying to highlight here is that the first fifteen minutes of your day, often overlooked, will have a big impact on your wellbeing and productivity for the remaining hours.

Set yourself up for success. Take ownership of the time, be mindful of your emotions and allow yourself to awake. These first fifteen minutes of your daily reset are crucial.

Make note below, on this page, what you do in the mornings and reflect on what you might redesign.

THE DOPAMINE TRAP

"If it's your job to eat a frog, it's best to do it
first thing in the morning. And if it's your job
to eat two frogs, it's best to eat the biggest
one first."

Mark Twain

It's easy to fall into the dopamine trap at the start of the workday. Crossing out simple tasks on our lengthy to-do list makes us feel good. The micro-dose of dopamine produced not only comes with feelings of accomplishment and satisfaction, it encourages us to keep going for more.

Yet, the check-box tasks are rarely the best use of our time when we start work. The 'low hanging fruit' may be easy to grab but is it the most nourishing? And just because something is presented as urgent, is it also important?

So rather than firing off some emails, finishing any task just to check it off, or responding to a request just because it's at the top of the pile, try to be more proactive in the morning—especially since you have the energy to tackle hard things. The easy things can be done later in the day when you're tired.

SEPTEMBER 4ᵀᴴ

ADDICTED TO DISTRACTION

"What information consumes is rather
obvious: it consumes the attention of its
recipients. Hence a wealth of information
creates a poverty of attention."

Herbert Simon

I t really hit home when I took the iPad away from my son and
he immediately went to the kitchen for a biscuit.

In many ways, technology is sugar for the brain. Some of the
neurological processes are surprisingly similar—and both are
highly addictive.

On an evolutionary level we became highly attuned to our
environment in order to scan for danger. New information was
rewarded with survival. The pings and red bubble notifications of
today's technology exploit this survival mechanism.

Technology addiction leads to a poverty of attention, more
distraction and a greater likelihood for multitasking. Some may
think we get more done by multitasking, but numerous studies
show that the time taken to complete a task increases as well as the
number of errors. Our brains are serial, not parallel, processors.

Whether or not you are an executive it's perhaps bearing
mind some classic wisdom from Peter Drucker in 1966:

"Effective executives do first things first, and one thing at a
time."

ADDICTED TO BUSY-NESS

"Music is the space between the notes."
Claude Debussy

I t was always the opening gambit on business small talk, at least pre-pandemic.

And I think there was always a reluctance to say we were not, actually, in response to the question, "busy"—as if it showed a sign of weakness, or even failure.

We tend to run from space in our non-working lives too, killing emerging signs of boredom with technology and other doing.

Yet the space is where the real value lies. The being and thinking, the not doing.

If someone asks if you are busy today, go ahead and say 'no'. Proudly.

DEEP WORK

How many hours do you expect to work today?

How many hours of that work do you expect to be uninterrupted, quality thinking time? With deep focus?

Check-box working, technology, distraction, multitasking, and being busy all prevent us from doing the deep work that gets results and gives us the greatest sense of accomplishment and wellbeing.

Former AOL CEO Tim Armstrong asked his executive team to spend 10% of their workday just thinking. Could you subscribe to that? That's more or less four hours a week.

In addition to taking time to think, how else could you improve your percentage of deep work today and this week? I've often felt a great sense of accomplishment on short-haul flights—two to three hours of uninterrupted work that I would love to replicate every non-travelling day.

Perhaps consider changing where you work, managing expectations, closing the door, wearing earphones. The head of the IDEO San Francisco studio worked, like everyone else, in an open plan office. He had a custom-built light above his desk. When this was switched on, everyone knew he was not to be disturbed.

Whatever it takes to work deeper, do it.

TIME FOR A SHOWER

Where do you do your best thinking?

Typical responses often include: during a daily commute, while exercising or walking the dog, just before sleeping, even in the shower. In many cases, anywhere and everywhere apart from the office!

I remember reading an article about a Silicon Valley entrepreneur who was so convinced that his best ideas came in the shower that he installed one in his office. His colleague then said to him: I don't know if you're getting any better ideas these days, but you're helluva clean!

Whatever you decide, try to formalise optimum thinking conditions within your day and give yourself permission to act on the fact that work, especially quality work, isn't simply desk time.

Any good thinking periods or ideas today? Note down when and where they happened below:

PEAKS AND VALLEYS

We all have two cognitive alertness peaks in a day: a primary and a rebound. Morning Larks will have their primary around 9:30 to 11:30am and evening Owls around 6:00 to 8:00pm. Each type, then, have their rebound peak in the primary period of the other.

Are you using these peaks wisely? For the evening, in particular, it's not that you should work, but it is an opportunity to use that time more intentionally.

Our daily low energy points are around 3pm and 3am. Beware what you schedule in the daytime 'nap-zone' and actively manage this low energy state, either by resting, energise through movement, or pick appropriate work.

Note below what you do today in each zone. Is it appropriate?

PEAK 1

VALLEY

PEAK 2

TAKE THE BREAK

W hat happens when you take a break at work?

The things you do—remain in active conversation or check your mobile device for emails, WhatsApps, and social media updates—might give you pleasure but not the full benefit of a break.

Depending on the intensity of the work you do, it's been shown that engaging in an activity where your cognitive load decreases is effective downtime.

And depending on your personality and the social nature of your job, chatting with co-workers can also help. Just be careful that what you talk about can affect the benefits if the conversation focuses on work!

Studies have also shown that calling or messaging a loved one boosts energy and mood, particularly in the afternoon.

I'm a big believer in simply getting outside and looking up at the sky. It's a good change to the typical work dynamic of inside and looking down.

WORK STARTS WHEN MEETINGS FINISH

How much of your day today will be taken up by meetings? (If you're reading this on the weekend, think of the working week you just finished).

I felt this was especially problematic during peak Working From Home mode at the beginning of the pandemic. Virtual back-to-back calls filled the day and people could only get stuff done after they had finished.

No-Meeting-Fridays were a late, only sometimes implemented and ultimately insufficient means of addressing the stressful accumulation of work piling up during the week.

I'd like to think that such extreme cases are starting to fade, yet meetings management is a critical consideration in your way of working. Think about some of the following:

- Try holding a face-to-face meeting with no technology.
- Don't accept the default half-hour or full hour when scheduling. Take back five minutes or seven. Anything.
- Start and finish meetings on time. Zero tolerance.
- Should everyone who *is* there *be* there? And should the meeting really take place?
- Ask someone in the meeting to help the group stick to the agenda, take notes, and follow up on actions.

continued to next page

continued from previous page

- Limit the amount of people in any meeting. Amazon follows the two-pizza rule, which should be enough to feed everyone present.
- Start a meeting with silent reading of a printed document, helping everyone present get on the same level for an informed discussion.

WHAT WILL YOU DO TO TAKE YOUR LIFE BACK FROM MEETINGS?

HOW TO DO VIRTUAL

Numerous studies show quite clearly that virtual teams are worse.

And better.

It depends on how they're used and in which context. I'm amazed after reflecting on my studies in virtual teams—having completed a PhD in the area in 2003—that the keys are still the same today: people are the core, technology is the add-on.

Don't try and replicate the face-to-face experience (even cutting the video feed can be valuable from time to time). It's a substitute, so manage your expectations. There's more 'noise' in the system—things in the way between sender and receiver which prevents clear communication.

I think there are three things needed to develop a base for going virtual. How well do you implement these online?

- The human touch, including patience and active listening.
- One-on-one dialogue to check understanding and address any red flags.
- Asking more meaningful questions to surface hidden needs and emotions.

WORKING FROM HOME OR LIVING AT WORK?

've spoken with hundreds of people who were abruptly pushed to 100% Working From Home mode as a result of the global pandemic.

Lots of people love it.

Lots of people hate it.

What is true for both extremes is that care is required to make the best out of the situation, ensuring we don't have a blurred work-life existence that results in a type of 'living at work' reality—in which work is always the primary concern, regardless of whether you are at home or in the corporate office. With the right approach, you can find and enjoy the benefits of both, wherever you happen to be working.

As many of us around the world settle into a more hybrid model of home and office, what is the best way to proceed? A good starting point is to think on things that should stay the same when Working From Home and things that should be different. Take a look at the below and see what else you can add:

Things that should stay the same
Getting dressed for work. The commute (or at least some time to transition from being at home to being at work). Making time for lunch.

Things that should be different
Always face-to-face meetings (cut the video and go for a walk and talk). Working at your desk (go where you feel best at different times of the day).

THE RULES OF THE GAME

Virtual is not the same as face-to-face. You can't simply proceed with the same rules of the game. A new protocol is needed, which serves as the 'guide-rails' for ensuring you keep moving forward, on track—especially when moving at high-speed.

Have a discussion with your team and think about some of the following:

- What are the key norms for virtual collaboration?
- How will reporting change for virtual work?
- Will the configuration of the team itself change? What happens if/when a new team member joins?
- What are the working hours and availability for virtual work? Is contact outside of these hours acceptable under certain circumstances?
- What are the communication channels we will use, and for what type of work?
- What are we happy doing virtually and what, if anything, must be done face-to-face?

A KEY TRANSITION

You'll transition from non-working life to working life today, and vice-versa. Maybe you're always in both worlds, but that is a discussion for another day.

When you return home and open the front door, or close the laptop and go to another room, perhaps to see your family, do you take work baggage with you?

Yes, sharing concerns and celebrations with loved ones is valuable, but take care with the energy you bring home from work.

Be more intentional with the switch between office and home. Is there a simple ritual, say a physical action or mantra, that will help you to make this transition?

THE FINAL 15 MINUTES

I t is the end of the day. You're tired. In the next 15 minutes (ideally) you'll be asleep and the day will be done. Time for a reset. What do you do?

If truth be told, I have wasted this time on checking email or social media but I am aware of the value of bidding adieu to my day in a more positive fashion. Some of the more useful practices I have found include:

Meditate

This may sound superfluous to some, but meditating is very different from sleeping (or trying to fall asleep). It calms the chaos of the day and readies you for sleep.

Reflect on your behaviour and actions

Sometimes a more active reflection on how your day is a useful option. Good or bad? Happy or sad? With pride or regret?

Read

I personally find this to be a powerful sleep aide, and have sometimes woken up the next morning to find the book still in bed! Just make sure you're reading a paperback (or at least a Kindle). Bright artificial, blue light will negatively impact your sleep.

Write in your journal

Give thanks, empty your mind, write plans for tomorrow. It's your journal.

How else could you spend this time?

HOW DID YOU SPEND YOUR DAY?

Fill in the following table for your working day today. Don't forget about non-digital reading and writing with your hand!

Activity	Time spent	Where does it take place?
Note any activities not listed	*Hours, Minutes OR High-Medium-Low*	*eg. office, park, home, commuting, long-haul travel, in the shower etc.*
Meetings		
Reading		
Writing		
Thinking		
Planning		
Emails		
_____ :		
_____ :		
_____ :		

FORGET WORKPLACE WELLNESS

There is a difference between wellness and wellbeing, although they are commonly used interchangeably. Wellness connotes some element of escape from the day-to-day reality and some notion of 'fixing'. Wellbeing, on the other hand, is a more integrated concept within the daily lived experience of human beings, which allows us to be well.

How we view this concept of wellbeing is critical if we are to change the prevailing culture in the workplace where wellbeing is something you do, or look after, on your own time and away from the office.

Working culture has often led to imbalance in employees' lives, and to address this the unsatisfied human needs of workers must be identified. Organizations must be rebuilt to embody wellbeing practices and ideology, rather than being the very thing that workers feel the need to escape from in search of 'wellness solutions'.

Forget workplace wellness. Workplace wellbeing is what we need.

UPSKILLING
(PART I)

remember some notes I sent to one of the senior partners at a large consulting firm just prior to the pandemic. I had delivered a wellbeing workshop to the young and exhausted associates and my notes read "I felt a lot of the comments pertained to core management and leadership skills, and so your wellbeing program could be used as a lens for improving, for example: prioritisation, managing upwards, managing downwards, communication, relationship building, and developing empathy, among others."

Wellbeing, and how we fit it into a busy professional life, is a necessary skill.

This became obvious to many during the pandemic because our working and our non-work lives became blurred. To take a technology analogy, we were forced to find a new operating system in order to manage the new way of working and living. Wellbeing skills include the ability to identify our deeper emotional needs, to design new routines and rituals, and to create a new system.

What wellbeing skills do you need to develop?

THE WAY YOU DO THINGS AROUND THERE

"Culture eats strategy for breakfast."

Peter Drucker

Culture may be defined as "the way we do things around here."

It's hard to grasp because it's mostly invisible. Yes, there is probably a policy, but the reality is mostly a feeling. So, how do you feel about your own workplace culture?

Is it *positive?* That is, do you feel that you are safe to be who you are and grow as a person at work?

Reflect on the following aspects of your workplace culture.

THINGS I LOVE.

THINGS I HATE.

HOW IT HAS CHANGED RECENTLY.

DESIGNING CULTURE

D an Strode couldn't believe Monday had rolled around again so fast. Sleep was at a premium during a busy 'working' weekend as a parent, but his mood lifted considerably when he entered his office and saw a small piece of paper on his desk. It read:

> *Good morning! Even the greatest weeks start*
> *with a Monday, so let's go for it!*

In that instant, Santander's global head of culture and strategy was energised. In that instant he looked forward to tackling the challenges of the day and week ahead. And he allowed himself just a little satisfaction that this note was part of a burgeoning positive company-wide culture that he had helped to design.

Dan and colleagues have attempted to design culture at a company of 202,000 employees through the *Santander Way*—eight behaviours that help guide daily action and provide clarity—*actively collaborate, bring passion, embrace change, keep promises, show respect, support people, talk straight,* and *truly listen.*

What behaviours would you like to see at your place of work?

TEAM AGREEMENTS

A team is a collection of people with diverse talents, each with individual preferences, who are able to work together. A high performing team flourishes on both difference and commonality. The whole is greater than the sum of its parts.

Try the following to create a platform for the way you work as a team.

- Imagine your team as a country and team members as its citizens. What behaviours define citizenship? What can you expect of each other, how do you hold each other accountable, and how can you set each other up for success and wellbeing?
- What are the functional needs of the team? (How you meet, communicate and report. The formal policies and procedures that keep you on track.)
- What are the personal needs of the team? (Individual needs and preferences.)
- What are the inspirational needs of the team? (The values and purpose you share. What drives you to aspire to excellent work?)

RELATIONSHIPS MATTER

You have friends at work. Or, you should have. The quality of relationships in the workplace not only impacts how you work but also your experience of work and overall wellbeing. Nothing gets done in a silo and constant collaboration is a hallmark of a thriving workplace.

- List below the most critical relationships in your place of work.
- Rate each from 1–5 where 1 is a complete lack of trust and avoidance, and 5 is deep enjoyment and great results.
- What can *you* do (it doesn't matter where the blame lies) to improve the score for each?

GREAT CONVERSATIONS

"The exchange of truth is curative. If you have a real conversation with someone, it will make both of you better."

Jordan Peterson

Relationships are defined by conversations. Improve the conversation and you'll improve the relationship. Reflect on the following questions for a specific relationship:

- Who talks the most in our conversations?
- Who is typically the subject of our conversations?
- Do I make a conscious effort to ask open questions—instead of rushing to give advice?
- Do I actively listen to learn?
- Do I show genuine interest and curiosity in the other party?
- How can I contribute more to celebrating the successes of the other person?
- Am I sometimes guilty of judging the other person in any way? Could I, instead, offer help?
- Which behaviours would I like to see more from my colleagues—and might I role-model them first?

START FINISHING
AND STOP STARTING

How many things will you work on today?

Of those, do you know when you started them?

For many, the answers to the above questions are 'too many' and 'long ago'. Crossing the finish line feels good. It gives us a sense of accomplishment, a reason to celebrate success and consider lessons learned for the future.

Starting is also good—new ideas, fresh energy, expectations of something new. Yet being caught in the middle, when energy inevitably wanes, creates a sense of drift which is exacerbated when this is replicated across numerous endeavours.

See what you can finish today, or at least plan for bringing it across that finish line soon.

Resist the temptation to start something new until you create some more space.

CHECKING IN, CHECKING OUT

C hecking in and out was a frequent proposition for some during the pre-pandemic world of work. Flights and hotels, then the currency of business travel, all called for our attention.

Now that business travel has paused, this concept of checking in and out is more important than ever. What do I mean? Well, many of us are drowning in a sea of endless back-to-back virtual meetings. Adding a check in and a check out to the start and stop of our daily interactions helps to prevent blurred vision and allows us to be more mindful. It will also keep team bonds strong and allow for you to take the emotional pulse of your colleagues and yourself.

Consider the following for your work interactions today. It can be done face-to-face, but is particularly critical for virtual work:

- Agree on taking the necessary time at the start and end of a meeting to check-in and check-out.
- Define the questions for checking-in. For example, *How am I feeling right now? Is there anything holding me back from being fully present?*
- Define the questions for checking-out. For example, *How am I feeling now? What is my main takeaway from this meeting?*
- Agree on who will do the check-in and check-out. For small meetings everyone may participate. In larger ones, a smaller selection.

This shouldn't be another thing to do in a busy day. Aim to make it voluntary and pleasant, surfacing rather than solving.

BUILDING TRUST

Trustworthiness = $\dfrac{\text{Credibility} + \text{Reliability} + \text{Intimacy}}{\text{Self-Orientation}}$

T rust is probably *the* foundational requirement for any high performing team. Without trust, results are simply not sustainable and conflict, when it inevitably arises, will scupper any notion of a collective.

Charles Green developed the above trust equation as a means of exploring the rational and emotional elements that comprise trust. Consider the following:

Credibility concerns truthfulness and believability. You can trust what someone says about a certain topic. Enhancing credibility includes doing the work, being open, and asking powerful questions. How might you increase your own credibility and that of your team?

Reliability concerns dependability and predictability. You can trust someone to do something. Enhancing reliability includes making and keeping promises. How might you increase your own reliability and that of your team?

Intimacy concerns discretion and empathy. You can trust someone with something. Enhancing intimacy includes being vulnerable and showing your emotions. How might you increase your own intimacy and that of your team?

Self-Orientation concerns motives and attention. You can trust that someone cares about more than themselves. Lowering self-orientation includes being curious, sharing your plans, and thinking out loud. How might you decrease your own self-orientation and that of your team?

DO YOU FEEL SAFE?

D o you feel safe at work?

I'm sure, for the majority of us, on a physical level that, yes, this is the case. Most organisations have long addressed any safety hazards that might present themselves during a working day.

Now, what about mentally and emotionally?

If you're not sure how to answer this question, think about the last time you made a mistake, or wanted to ask a question but felt it was too simple or obvious. Maybe you were ready to share an idea but didn't think it was a good one. We're all reluctant to engage in behaviours that could negatively influence how others perceive our competence, awareness, and positivity.

Yet, we move forward together by learning from mistakes. The simple or obvious question you decided not to ask in the end was probably on the lips of every single one of your colleagues. As for ideas, history's greatest innovations have been built on the simplest and craziest of insights.

How can you increase psychological safety for yourself and for others? We've talked about it over the course of this month.

Be more curious, more open, more empathetic, more explorative, more collaborative.

BELONGING

The Minister for Development arrives at the office by bicycle and gets straight to work. Meeting the other ministries is first on the agenda today, with a number of initiatives in the offing to improve the day-to-day lives of the 400 people that make up the Republic. The Minster for Health and Wellbeing kicks of the meeting, with some particularly good ideas coming from the Minister for Parties and Good Times.

You will have realised by now that this is not your conventional set of government ministries. It is an innovative cultural initiative at the UK telco giffgaff. The aim is to create a sense of belonging and emotional connection to something special, where culture is also created from the bottom up rather than dictated by management. giffgaff has a set of carefully curated values designed by management: curiosity, collaboration, grit, and positivity—and the ministries help bring people closer together in alignment with these.

There is advantage in difference within the workplace. Inclusion ensures that people aren't punished for being different and a sense of belonging.

Do you feel like you belong?

PROGRESS OVER PERFECTION

A t the time of writing *The Daily Reset* my son is six. He has created a lot of mess in the last year or two. He calls it his 'experiments'. It usually involves mixing water and whatever other object or liquid is nearby.

Children are naturally curious and playful and they learn through doing. As adults, we tend to become fixed and serious and we shy away from practice. Let me give you an example.

The Marshmallow Challenge is a popular activity whereby teams have fifteen minutes to construct the highest tower made of dry spaghetti that will support a marshmallow on top. MBA students are terrible at this challenge. They overthink it, they plan, and they only place the marshmallow on the top when the end of the allocated time has neared—and when the tower inevitably falls.

Little kids on the other hand are great at it. They have no pretensions of success. They start with building a tiny tower, place the marshmallow on top and celebrate. Then they build it higher. And higher. They learn by doing. They experiment.

Are you concerned with mess at work? Or do you strive for getting it right first time? We learn more through mess. We learn more through failure. We learn more through trying something new.

Try it out today. Aim for progress over perfection.

LIFE/WORK

T he First Industrial Revolution treated people like machines and created a sun-up to sun-down working day that even took children out of school just to keep up with demand. One of the first experiments in creating a more human workplace was the cotton mills of New Lanark, 20 miles from where I grew up in Scotland. The manager of the mills (which had the world's first nursery school) Robert Owen, promoted a balanced daily life that included "eight hours' labour, eight hours' recreation, and eight hours' rest."

Today, work-life balance continues to raise fierce debate. The pandemic made people question it in their own life and employers are now looking for ways to improve it for their workforce.

We've considered different ways of working this month. This is part of the conversation about ways of living. Better ways of working will create a better way of living.

As you've reflected on your own working life this month, and will no doubt continue to do so, I leave you with one final thought.

Instead of calling it work-life balance, shouldn't we flip the order?

What's the best life-work balance for you?

NOTES ON YOUR JOURNEY THROUGH
WAYS OF WORKING IN SEPTEMBER:

WAYS OF WORKING

OCTOBER

RESILIENCE

BOUNCEBACKABILITY

I've used the term *bouncebackability* to talk about resilience over the years. The word seems to resonate with people because it is descriptive and visual. I don't even know where I picked it up, but it entered the Oxford English Dictionary in 2005 and is credited to former Crystal Palace footballer Iain Dowie who hailed his teams 'bouncebackability' in recovering from defeat in the earlier part of the season to then go on to the English Premier League.

To broaden an understanding of resilience, I complement the term with a definition from US researcher Andrew Zolli: *how to help vulnerable people, organizations and systems persist, perhaps even thrive, amid unforeseeable disruptions.*

I do think, though, that disruptions for the most part can be foreseen (though we don't always act). And you may not consider yourself to be vulnerable either, but all in all Zolli's definition is useful. At some point in our lives, we all need resilience. Wherever you are right now in your journey, or whatever interpretation you have of resilience, let's consider bouncing back this month.

REFLECTIONS ON THE ROLLERCOASTER

March 2020 was the start of a wild ride. I spent some dark days thinking my business might not survive the pandemic. All our bookings for the year at The Leadership Academy of Barcelona literally disappeared overnight.

And yet, I also recall that time with a certain fondness. I was at home with my family and felt grateful for that safety in the midst of global chaos.

Not that it wasn't chaotic at home. Trying to work with a home-schooling five-year-old spinning around the apartment who, given Spanish Government restrictions, didn't leave the house for six long weeks was difficult to say the least. The add-on was a three-month old Sheepdog, and all that puppy mess to clean up.

But, what I realized was that each of these difficulties came with their own goodness. The puppy gave me official permission to enjoy short walks in the middle of a deserted, peaceful city. Being at home with my son meant I was there to experience him reading and writing for the first time. And on top of that, although business remained fragile, I was later humbled to learn at the end of the year that it was our highest turnover since starting trading in 2007.

Ups and downs. I became more comfortable than ever before with both.

What were yours?

THE STOCKDALE PARADOX

"I never lost faith in the end of the story. I never doubted not only that I would get out, but also that I would prevail in the end and turn the experience into the defining event of my life."

Admiral James Bond Stockdale

James Stockdale was a US pilot who was a prisoner of war in Hanoi, Vietnam for eight years where he was routinely tortured. In the business book *Good to Great*, James Collins writes about a conversation he had with Stockdale regarding his coping strategy during this period, which gave rise to the Stockdale Paradox: *the appreciation of one's brutal reality, but with an all-powerful positive vision.*

Stockdale added that "You must never confuse faith that you will prevail in the end—which you can never afford to lose—with the discipline to confront the most brutal facts of your current reality, whatever they might be."

When people said to me that the pandemic-ravaged year of 2020 should be confined to the dust-bin, I encouraged them to drill deeper on their experience. For some, it may even be, like Stockdale, the defining event of their life.

What about you?

LEMONS AND LEMONADE

S tuff happens. Bad stuff. To everyone. All the time.
Here's the key: don't make it worse.
There is reality, and there is our response to that reality.
We can make things better, and we can make things worse. Too
often, we can even make them significantly worse through our
reaction and subsequent actions.

If something happens to you today that isn't welcome or positive, think about how you can make it better. At the very least
don't be the source of making it worse.

BE THE PERSON ON THE BOAT

"In Vietnam, there are many people, called
boat people, who leave the country in small
boats. Often the boats are caught in rough
seas or storms, the people may panic, and
boats can sink. But if even one person aboard
can remain calm, lucid, knowing what to do
and what not to do, he or she can help the
boat survive. His or her expression—face,
voice—communicates clarity and calmness,
and people have trust in that person. They will
listen to what he or she says. One such person
can save the lives of many."

Thich Nhat Hanh

Thich Nhat Hanh is a Vietnamese Buddhist monk and peace
activist. This powerful passage comes from the experience
of the Vietnamese boat people who cross the Gulf of Siam.
This is not about hiding from your true feelings. Rather, it is
focused on how behaviour and mindset are among the most contagious things in society. We pick up on even the subtlest of cues.

Try being the person on the boat today, especially if today is
a day that you find yourself caught in a 'rough sea or storm'.

You'll find that the calmness and tranquillity that transmits
to those around you comes back to reinforce your own feelings.

BE CAREFUL WHAT YOU PAY ATTENTION TO

"What you attend to in this moment becomes your reality."

William James

W hat we pay attention to affects our mindset.
If all we consume is alarmist news channels that focus on bad news, we will become alarmist and filled with fear.

If all we consume is escapist social media memes, we may be entertained for a while, but will have no grasp on reality.

A resilient mindset is cultivated by balancing these extremes.

Be mindful of what you pay attention to today. How does it make you feel?

IRIGOYEN'S DAILY

n the year 1929, and nearing the end of his second, ill-fated, term as President of Argentina, Hipólito Irigoyen began to receive filtered news from his closest aides. The Great Depression was having a devastating impact throughout Latin America and the country was sliding inexorably into crisis. This highlighting of only good news and passing over the more negative events in communication with the president led to one of Argentina's most popular myths: that a special newspaper was printed for Irigoyen that featured only good news. *El Diario de Irigoyen* (or Irigoyen's Daily), is a well-known phrase in Argentina to this day, and used when people want to push back against the "sugar-coated" version of events.

We can all be tempted to create our own Irigoyen's Daily, especially when things are tough. We may enjoy the solace and escapism in the short term but it does nothing for our long-term resilience.

Confront reality. No matter how hard it may be, it is easier when taken a day at a time. Go for the daily reset.

TWO CIRCLES

G rowing up in a working-class household in the West of Scotland in the 1980s I was puzzled, even at a very early age, at two things my father did. More specifically, two things that he complained about.

First, he complained incessantly about the weather.

Second, he complained even more about Margaret Thatcher.

I subsequently found out that these were the complaints du jour of countless households across the country. But, to what end? Can we change the weather? Putting aside questions of climate change, strictly speaking, no. Ousting Thatcher from her role as UK Prime Minister? There were political intricacies here which make this, surprising as it may seem for a modern democracy, an equal no.

I have huge empathy for the attitude of my father, and perhaps there was value in being able to vent, but he was literally wasting his breath.

Reactive people have a large circle of concern and a small circle of control. A lot of time and energy is wasted reacting to things they can't control.

Proactive people have a small circle of concern and a large circle of control. A lot of time and energy is focused on issues that are within their control.

Today, you have limited time and energy. How will you spend it?

TACKLING YOUR
WORRY LIST

T ry this today, perhaps even in the space available on this page.

List all the things that are worrying you right now.

Place a tick next to those fully within your control.

Place a question mark next to those you may be able to influence.

Place an X next to those out of your control.

This is your energy and attention plan.

IT'S OK TO...
MAKE YOUR OWN RULES

'It's ok not to be ok' has been a cornerstone of mental health advice for years, and was frequently used during the worst stages of the pandemic.

In 2016, Giles Turnbull from the UK Government Digital Service wrote a 'It's ok to...' list that was designed primarily for new hires to absorb the culture of the workplace quickly and easily. Among the 34 things on the list, which was posted widely around the office, are:

- Say "I don't know"
- Ask why, and why not
- Ask for help
- Make mistakes
- Sing
- Sigh
- Not check your email out of hours
- Have off-days
- Have days off

At a time when we all might feel the pressure to follow rules that no longer apply, this list serves as a fantastic reminder that it's ok to make our own rules.

What might your own 'it's ok to...' list look like?

TWO TYPES OF STRESS

"It's not stress that kills us, it is our reaction to it."
Hans Selye

Stress gets a bad rap. It shouldn't. At least, not all the time. It's also poorly understood. Stress is the physiological response to an external event, a *stressor*. Increased heart rate, clammy palms, shallow breath, these may all be a result of that stressor.

Hungarian-Canadian endocrinologist Hans Selye pioneered the study of stress in the early 1940s, later defining two distinct types: eustress (good stress) and distress (bad stress). Studies show that eustress is critical for overall wellbeing.

It's not strictly the case that eustress is a particular type of event (or stressor) and distress another, but rather how we perceive it. The circumstances of the particular event also matter, as in the timing, how prepared we are, and how long it lasts.

For example, physical exercise, learning, a deadline at work, an unexpected occurrence, these can all be beneficial in one context—we become stronger, more knowledgeable, agile, and adaptable. However, these same things can also lead to fatigue, anxiety, feeling overwhelmed, and burnout.

Try not to be automatically triggered when a stressor presents itself today (and it will). Think about what can you do to make it eustress instead of distress.

STRESS IS YOUR FRIEND

C an we make stress our friend?

Health psychologist Kelly McGonigal posed this question in her 2013 TED Talk. Seven distinct areas of research were highlighted:

- Stress correlates to a lower risk of death when we *perceive* it as having no negative health impact, regardless of the quantity of stress.
- Stress boosts the production of neurons that can improve mental performance.
- Bursts of stress can strengthen the immune system, by producing supportive hormones through the adrenal glands.
- Stress can make you more social, and increase levels of trust and sharing.
- Some types of stress can improve learning, with one study showing the benefit of cold water for improving test scores.
- Stress can improve memory. We recall stressful events, good or bad, in our lives.
- Stress may help you connect with your instincts, with test subjects doing better on tasks which were less about the details and more about going with your gut.

If you encounter stress today think about how it can be your friend.

COLD SHOWERS

I waited nervously as the end of the song approached. The beats of the next one kicked in and I immediately pushed the shower handle to the opposite side. A blast of ice-cold water shocked my body and I started to dance around to the music. The dancing took my mind off the freezing water and I just made it to the end of the song. After two years of failed attempts at cold showers this was the starting point for a now eighteen-month-old daily ritual I can't do without.

There is a growing body of research that shows the benefits of cold water, including decreased inflammation and improved mood, focus, and weight and energy management. Those cold showers were an important coping mechanism for me at the beginning of the pandemic.

Now there's no need for the dancing or songs. I have a very meditative response to the stressor of the cold water and am now much more resilient to it.

Essentially, I *practiced* the stress response. My 'fight-or-flight' mechanism kicked in at the beginning and my response was to fight (active dancing) where previously it had been flight (turn off the cold water). After time, I was better able to manage this response, and no longer need to 'fight'. Not only has this improved my cold-water response, but I'm now better able to manage the 'fight-or-flight' mechanism when it happens in other areas of my life.

Try a cold shower today. It's not easy. But it will get easier.

And it might just change your life.

THE STRESS EQUATION

Growth = Stress + Recovery

Stress is valuable—allowing us to develop and learn—but it must be followed by recovery if it is to work to our advantage: muscle fibres break during weight training then grow back stronger afterwards. A similar process occurs with the heart during cardiovascular exercise. We land the learning after a period of study.

Without the space, rest and recovery after the 'work' or load of stress, we don't take full advantage of it.

We can grow through stress. Just don't forget about the recovery.

REFRAMING

S tudies in human happiness typically look at two dimensions. They first consider how people feel right now in the moment and then, how satisfied they are looking back on their life

With the passing of time, we often view things in a different light. Reframing is an immensely valuable part of our daily human experience.

Let's try it now.

- Think about a really bad day in the past few weeks or months.
- Is there a positive element you can take from that now?
- How might that change your mindset the next time you encounter a 'bad' experience?

THE POWER OF GRATITUDE

Expressing gratitude is one of the simplest and most powerful tools at our disposal. It's good for our bodies and our minds. Studies show the benefits to include increased happiness, optimism, and positive emotions, a stronger immune system, lower blood pressure, better sleep, and improved focus and determination to achieve ones' goals. Recent research has even found that gratitude changes the prefrontal cortex area of the brain, which may support mental health in the longer term.

Keeping a gratitude journal is a common practice. Perhaps you express your gratitude to another person or engage in a benevolent act.

Or you can just self-reflect, at the beginning or the end of your day: what do you have, right now, in your life that you are grateful for?

HAVING A LAUGH

There is a member of my family who has had a tough time of it for an extended number of years. But she loves to laugh. I've often reflected that this is a hugely important coping mechanism for her.

Studies show that a sense of humour is a key contributor to resilience. It is one of several positive character traits, including kindness, generosity, curiosity, and love, which have the capacity to grow significantly in response to major trauma, and are also traits which predict higher levels of life satisfaction.

Humour is also a key release for those engaged in a setting of continual trauma, such as fire, police, and medical professionals, particularly those working in an Emergency Room situation. One of the reasons may be that humour creates a safe buffer between the trauma and pain they witness and their own wellbeing.

Whatever happens to you today, or for the next personal trauma you face, are you able to find a funny side?

Or maybe just laugh. See how you feel.

BREATHE IT OUT

Cortisol is the stress hormone, which is produced as part of our daily rhythm. For example, cortisol levels peak shortly after waking so as to give us the necessary 'oomph' to get going. It is also produced in response to a perceived threat, as part of the 'fight-or-flight' mechanism. Once the alarm to release cortisol has been sounded, your body becomes mobilized and ready for action! But, if we don't appropriately engage with our fight or flight reactions, a build-up of cortisol can cause a variety of health problems.

Breathing can help.

Just three minutes of deep, controlled, belly breathing can change the part of your nervous system responsible for 'fight-or-flight'.

Try the following during a stressful situation, or as soon after as possible to recover.

- Lie on your back, shoes off, with your knees bent and feet flat on the floor. If lying down isn't possible, sit comfortably with your feet firmly on the ground.
- Place both hands on your belly.
- Close your eyes and inhale deeply through your nose to the count of four. Aim for maximum movement of your belly.
- Exhale through your mouth to the count of four. Feel the movement of your belly.
- Maintain this rhythm for as long as you feel necessary. Try it for one minute at least.

THE HEALING POWER OF NATURE

The first few months of pandemic lockdown in Barcelona were difficult. We were not permitted to leave the house, save to go out for essential supplies. It did have its benefits however. I'll never forget the feeling of peace that came from being in the middle of a large city in absolute quiet—no people, no cars. Sitting on my balcony in the Spring sunshine and listening to much louder birdsong was a special moment, and reminded me of the great healing power of the great outdoors and of the important fact that we are part of nature and nature is part of us.

Many experts believe, from a genetic standpoint at least, that we are no different from the hunter-gatherers of 40,000 years ago and are meant to live in nature. Do you remember being fascinated by any rural element as a child? Exploring and looking for treasure perhaps? What about vacation and the deep nourishment that came from watching the sunrise or sunset?

Many modern-day illnesses, including those within the domain of mental health, can be attributed to a lack of contact with nature. For this reason, there are now a number of buildings that include elements of biophilia—the presence of nature—to make us feel better when we're in them.

How much have you connected with nature in recent weeks or even in the past few days? How can you get a little closer today?

DAILY CONNECTION

I spent an unforgettable weekend in the wilderness of the Slovenian Alps with McKinsey's Aberkyn in July 2018. It was hugely restorative but not exactly feasible on a regular basis. So what are other ways that we can connect with nature?

Walk among trees
Maybe you hate hiking or camping, or simply don't have the time. Look for a local park. Research shows that walking within natural elements has positive benefits for mental health, reducing blood flow to the part of the brain responsible for rumination, a specific type of stress when we tend to fixate on an issue or problem.

Get a houseplant
Going outdoors is ideal, but we can bring the outside in too—especially since we spend up to 90% of our lives inside a building. Studies have shown that adding houseplants to an otherwise sparse space can increase wellbeing, creativity, and productivity by around 40%.

Look out the window
Studies have shown hospital patients recover more quickly when exposed to natural light from a window. Take the break. Lift your attention from your own worries and see the natural world around you.

FIRE

We need fire in our lives.

If you light a candle, you may awaken the primal instinct of sitting around a fire and connect with your ancestral self. I've found lighting a candle to be a hugely relaxing ritual.

And we need the sun. That ball of fire in the sky regulates our daily rhythm through light and dark cycles, which is especially important in an age with continual exposure to artificial light and digital devices.

The sun is also our biggest source of Vitamin D, necessary for strong bones, muscles, and teeth.

Where will you get your fire today?

If you want to consider the metaphorical view of fire, in line with some views from ancient philosophy, what are your passions and desires? What energises you?

WATER

"Empty your mind, be formless, shapeless—
like water. Now you put water in a cup,
it becomes the cup; you put water in a bottle
it becomes the bottle; you put it in a teapot it
becomes the teapot. Now water can flow or it
can crash. Be water, my friend."

Bruce Lee

We need water in our lives.

Up to 60% of the human adult body is water (we are 'wetter' when born, around 75%). It serves a critical function in all areas of the body including the production of neurotransmitters in the brain, the delivery of oxygen throughout the body, and the flushing of waste. Maintaining good hydration is key for both physical and mental health. We need between two and three litres per day.

I also think being close to water or observing water has huge benefits—think about the sense of calm observing a still lake or the exhilaration of a crashing wave or noisy waterfall!

Immersion in water is special too, perhaps taking us back to our time in the womb. A bath or shower is a daily functional act and can be a restorative ritual.

How will you get your water today?

If you want to consider the metaphorical view of water, in line with some views from ancient philosophy, how does what you do flow to other people? What is your legacy and contribution to others?

AIR

W e need air in our lives.

Fresh air for starters. I've become increasingly worried about the levels of air pollution in the city of Barcelona where I live and am paying more attention to different measurements and policy from the local government to address air quality. It's a challenge in urban centres around the world where companies are now looking at air quality as part of an overall push on healthy buildings.

Good ventilation was also a major factor in combatting the spread of COVID-19. For example, a formal part of German government policy to tackle the pandemic built on the strong culture of *lüften* where Germans have long had a daily practice of recycling household air through opening windows.

And if you're able to enjoy a place with clean fresh air, breathe deeply.

How will you get your air today?

If you want to consider the metaphorical view of air, in line with some views from ancient philosophy, what is your unique voice or spirit? What sets you apart in all the daily chaos and how can you find and stay true to your uniqueness?

EARTH

We need earth in our lives.
I've found gardening to be a highly therapeutic practice, not to mention digging my hands into the soil reminds me of the fun I had digging in the dirt as a child!

Earth in our diet also contributes to good health, so consider how many things you eat which grow in the earth. Some people also choose to take a clay supplement to deal with inflammation.

And give *earthing* a try, as a means of connecting with the earth. Simply walk or stand barefoot. Feel the grass, sand, dirt, whatever the surface is. A friend had a terrible time calming her young baby, and tried everything to no avail until she discovered that what worked was walking barefoot on the grass in a local park.

How will you get your earth today?

If you want to consider the metaphorical view of earth, in line with some views from ancient philosophy, what are your values and principles? Your ethics? What grounds you and where are you headed?

LOST AND FOUND

*T*he *Daily Reset* is about our life journey. The path we follow each and every day. We don't always know where we're going or when we arrive. We learn as we go.

I've been a runner most of my life. I've raced a lot of track and road races, but I feel most alive in deep nature, often with no fixed idea where I'm going. I'm lucky to live on the edge of a large natural park, Parc Collserola on the upper edge of Barcelona.

One of the biggest benefits is the huge range of paths or *corriols*—narrow, sinewy inclines and descents that serve as alternatives to the main path. Running along the main path is usually complemented by these alternatives, as long as I lift my gaze and pay attention to what's going on around me. These alternatives can offer new ways of arriving at the same destination or present a new end point. Often, they lead to a dead-end and I need to go back. The joy is in the discovery. Getting lost and finding myself again.

LOWER YOUR MASK

For more than a year I wore a mask every time I left my home. On the streets of Barcelona everyone has one. And it makes it harder to communicate with people, to read their emotions. One of the basic, most valued gestures of human connection, the smile, has sadly disappeared from view.

This hiding of emotions got me thinking of how we often do the same in a metaphorical sense, 'putting a brave face on things'—most of us tend to keep it inside, without sharing our problems with others.

To cultivate resilience it helps to be vulnerable.

Share your own concerns and fears. Open up. With your family and friends, of course. Yet maybe you could also consider your workplace. Share an issue that has been bothering you. If you're nervous of doing this first, think about how you might pay attention to, and help others who might be vulnerable.

How might you lower your mask today?

BE A LEARN-IT-ALL

A lack of resilience may be associated with a sense of power-lessness. The feeling that we're victims to circumstance. Learning empowers us.

We can take control of our destiny. At the very least our intention and attention. Through our actions, we play an active rather than passive role in our lives. We energise ourselves by being engaged in a search for answers. We may even apply what we learn to future scenarios where our resilience is tested. We grow.

How might you feed your curiosity today? What should you pay attention to?

What will you learn?

LOVE LEARNING

'm 44 years old and just bought my first-ever skateboard. My six-year-old son got one and we decided to learn together.

We hear so much about the need to make space for learning these days but I don't think it needs to be limited to 'work stuff'.

Coordination and balance are critical factors that wane as we age and I think the neuroplasticity benefits of my modest skateboarding attempts (ie: skate a few metres without falling off!) are as powerful as any more 'cerebral' learning.

I'm loving being a novice at something—the quick wins and early progress. Loving spending time with my son. Loving the learning.

THE FORMULA FOR GOOD MENTAL HEALTH

Our biochemistry has a huge effect on our mental health and resilience. Here are two elements to be aware of and actions you can take today to find the right formula for good mental health.

Serotonin is the wellbeing hormone and one of the brain's key neurotransmitters (the chemical 'messengers'). It is responsible for the regulation of mood, aggression, appetite, and sleep.

- Good habits go a long way. Exercise and protein-rich foods including eggs, nuts, and salmon help promote serotonin production. Sunlight also increases serotonin levels—indeed *any* daylight—so get outside!

Dopamine is the reward hormone and plays a role in many forms of addiction, from drugs and food, to modern-day 'addictions' like social media.

- Try a dopamine 'fast' by decreasing your time scrolling through different social media feeds. Rearranging your phone apps and changing your screen to greyscale will also result in more intentional, less mindless, smartphone use.

YOU ARE MORE THAN
YOUR ACCOMPLISHMENTS

One of the biggest stories of the 2020 Tokyo Olympics was the withdrawal of US gymnast Simone Biles. Along with Japanese Tennis player Naomi Osaka, she was considered the face of the Games akin to, say, Usain Bolt or Michael Phelps from previous Olympiads.

Her bravery was remarkable. The pressure globally, and particularly in the US, to perform and add to her already historic achievements as the world's greatest gymnast, was immense.

But she knew it would be dangerous to continue. The easy choice perhaps, but very dangerous. The 'twisties' she talked about—of not having any sense of awareness during tumbles and vaults—could have had life-threatening consequences.

She talked extensively about her decision before coming back to earn a brave Bronze medal in the individual beam. Showing remarkable self-assuredness for a young woman who was also subject to sexual abuse in the US gymnastics set-up at a young age she said, "I am more than my accomplishments."

In a world of increasing pressure and perfectionism, I think that is worth remembering.

BE KIND TO YOURSELF

Experts say that William Shakespeare wrote *King Lear* in one of the frequent London lockdowns of the early 17th century when the city was frequently ravaged by the plague.

In my own Barcelona lockdown of March 2020 I witnessed my five-year-old son learning to read and write for the first time, in his non-native language (Catalan), via Zoom.

You may be aware of people in your life who tackled big challenges during the pandemic in spite of the many restrictions we all faced. They are deserving of recognition, yes, but it's important not to fall into the comparison game.

Give yourself a break.

I think it's enough to reflect on what you have learned about yourself in recent times. Give yourself a pat on the back. You deserve it.

NOTES ON YOUR JOURNEY THROUGH
RESILIENCE IN OCTOBER:

NOVEMBER

LEADERSHIP

LEADERSHIP IS ABOUT OTHERS

[MY JOURNAL]

An egotistical form of leadership has become the norm as of late, forgoing the simple fact that leadership is about others.

It is not about you. It is about how you may help other people develop so that they, in turn, can become leaders and create positive change. Servant Leadership is a philosophy over a half a century old which may prove to be useful in our post-pandemic world. In 1970, its creator Robert K. Greenleaf asked the following question:

Do those served grow as persons? Do they, while being served, become healthier, wiser, freer, more autonomous, more likely themselves to become servants?

Ask yourself the question today as we begin our journey this month in leadership.

[YOUR JOURNAL]

LEADERS ARE HUMANS TOO

The Telefónica CEO José María Álvarez-Pallete López told me a few years ago: *"It's not like I lead only with my head at work and only with my heart at home. I'm the same person in both places."*

How can you bring more alignment into your life? The greater the distance between who we are depending on where we are, the more tiring it is to maintain.

Perhaps there is an assumption that who we are in our personal life isn't 'professional' enough, whatever that means. I think the new world of work demands character traits that will serve us well no matter where we are on a daily basis.

Empathy, listening, healing, awareness, foresight, building community, and a commitment to the growth of people all allow us to be true leaders at home and in the office.

EMOTIONS AT WORK

How much of your emotional self do you bring to work? We tend to let our rational selves dominate our work persona—and this is not always a bad thing, but emotions used well can improve a variety of leadership elements.

When we share some of our own emotions at work, rather than sticking with our rational side, we draw others towards us, building loyalty and trust and this is what gets us through the tough times.

Life, and work, is an emotional rollercoaster. Surrendering to those extremes doesn't allow us to go where we want to go, but neither can we tame them completely.

What happens with your own team? Think about how you celebrate the wins and learn from the losses. There will be waves of highs and lows. Learn how to surf.

IT'S NOT A POPULARITY CONTEST

"If we wish to help humans to become more
fully human, we must realize not only that they
try to realize themselves, but that they are also
reluctant or afraid or unable to do so."

Abraham Maslow

Many leaders want to be loved, and many are. But a desire to be liked shouldn't guide decision making.

Leadership is about developing others and organisations. And development can be painful. It involves asking the tough questions, pushing people to confront the things they are perhaps unwilling to confront themselves, stretching them to be the best they can be. Ask yourself about the greater good, the longer-term development goals, and don't shy away from the tough calls.

Remember this the next time you need to make a leadership decision.

It might make you unpopular, but what if it is the right thing to do?

WE ALL LEAD

One December evening in 1955, Rosa Parks got the bus home after work in the US city of Montgomery. When all the segregated white seats at the front of the bus filled up, the bus driver ordered her to give up her seat, in the first row designated for black people. She refused to do so, and her case became a pivotal moment in the civil rights movement.

She had no authority. But she led.

Maybe you have a formal leadership role at work. If you don't, that doesn't mean you can't practice leadership.

These days, many organisations are less hierarchical and encourage good leadership practice from all employees, regardless of experience or role. Everyone can lead by example. The things you say, the things you do, the way you act and live your day to day, these all impact the people you come into contact with.

We lead in different parts of our lives too, not just at work. You have a role as a daughter or son, brother or sister, friend and parent.

We all lead, or at least we have the option to do so. Every day.

DEPLOYING YOUR SKILLS

"Don't reserve your best business thinking for your career."

Clayton Christensen

What do you do for a living? It's likely that you've practiced your art, whatever that may be, for a significant amount of time. Time on its own, practice, this tends to result in significant skill development. Add in formal company training and learning from others and this practice becomes elevated and you will have highly specialised skills in a specific area.

I'm sure that you're very capable of successfully implementing those skills in your place of work. That's what you're paid for after all.

How about taking those same skills to other areas of your life?

Perhaps you already do it without thinking, but by bringing more attention to the deployment of your work skills into other parts of your life, you just might learn more about yourself, further develop those skills, and make a positive impact on others.

PUT YOUR OWN MASK ON FIRST

t's likely you're not flying around these days as much as you used to. It's projected that the airline industry won't recover to 2019 levels before 2024. But you know the drill. In order to take better care of those around you, you put your own oxygen mask on first.

Do you make time for yourself? Do you take care of your health? Or are you running yourself into the ground with work and your duties in other parts of your life?

- How much time do you invest in your physical health and wellbeing every week?
- How much time do you invest in your mental health and wellbeing every week?
- How much time do you invest in your emotional health and wellbeing every week?
- How much time do you invest in your spiritual health and wellbeing every week?

Taking care of yourself is the best way of taking care of others, in both your private and professional life.

THEY'RE LOOKING AT YOU

> "We but mirror the world. All the tendencies
> present in the outer world are to be found
> in the world of our body. If we could change
> ourselves, the tendencies in the world would
> also change."
>
> *Mahatma Ghandi*

I f you're the most senior person in the room, people look at you six times more.

What an opportunity.

Role modelling is a hugely important part of leadership. It can help define behaviour and culture in an organisation. It will encourage people to change. Whether it's young employees who aspire to a leadership position or simply those who admire who you are, in whatever part of your life (think of parenting, for example). Knowing this should make us more mindful of our own behaviour.

The things you do today. The things you say. You may notice others doing and saying the same things soon.

YOUR LEGACY
IS OTHER PEOPLE

What will be the lasting legacy of your leadership? Perhaps it will be measurable business results, how your organisation succeeds in the market compared to competitors. This, however, may be temporary. In comparison, the greater impact, the one that lasts, is other people. How they act and change as a result of being in contact with you.

Mentorship is hugely important. Everyone, no matter who they are, can benefit from a mentor. And the value is often a two-way street. Mentees flourish with the guidance and external view from someone with experience and mentors not only see the result of their hard work over years manifested in the best possible place—another human being—but also have the chance to gain a new perspective and even learn something new too.

How might you positively guide and nurture someone else today?

Is it time to become a formal mentor to someone who could benefit from your wisdom and experience?

Regardless of any formal mechanism, look for role-models in your life, and strive to be a role-model to others.

ECOSYSTEM OVER EGOSYSTEM

re you part of an ecosystem or an egosystem? Which one do you help create?

EGO SYSTEM	ECO SYSTEM	Where are you?
"This is about me"	*"This is about everyone"*	
Control from above	*Self-organization*	
Independence	*Interdependence*	
Command	*Conversation*	
Territorial	*Collaborative*	
Power struggles	*Empower everyone*	
Self-interest	*Mutual support*	
Withhold information	*Transparency and sharing*	
Blame	*Mutual responsibility*	

VULNERABILITY IS STRENGTH

Vulnerability does not equate with weakness. It is a sign of strength. As the COVID-19 pandemic accelerated in March 2020, the Marriott Hotels CEO Arne Sorenson published a video message on Twitter talking of the huge crisis facing the company which was, in his words "worse than the 2007 economic crisis and the September 11 World Trade Center attacks combined." He showed real emotion in his address, coming close to tears on several occasions. Even his appearance, bald from undergoing cancer treatment, was an exercise in showing vulnerability. The message was hailed on all sides as the type of leadership necessary to navigate the crisis.

When we increase transparency, empathy, and emotion—all evident in Sorenson's address—we help to build a culture of psychological safety, and studies show this helps to build the strong team bonds and engagement that results in high performance.

How can you show more vulnerability today?

How can you share with others that it's ok to bring their true, whole selves to work?

NOT KNOWING

"Google values the ability to take a step back and adopt the ideas of other people if they are better. It is about having 'intellectual humility.' Without humility it is impossible to learn."
Lazlo Bock, Ex VP People Ops Google

I t used to be that leaders were the ones with all the answers. The people that others would go to for help with an important question or problem.

Maybe that is still the case. Leaders often have more experience, more time in the world of work, from which answers and solutions may present themselves.

Nowadays, however, the world is moving so fast that this isn't always so. And this change can be scary for a leader.

What do you do? Pretend you have the answer? Bluff your way out of it? Perhaps it's time to acknowledge that leaders are orchestrators rather than experts.

Embrace the fuzzy nature of work. Lean into it and find out the answers together rather than pretending you know everything. It's not a sign of weakness.

PRACTICING HUMBLE LEADERSHIP

How should a leader impact those around them? Lead by example? Yes. Motivate and inspire? Absolutely. To do all this, it is not necessary to be an extrovert. It is true that many leaders are indeed extroverts, but introverts make excellent leaders too.

Studies show that higher performing teams are increasingly being led by humble leaders. Humble people tend to be aware of their own weaknesses, are eager to improve themselves, appreciative of others' strengths and focused on goals beyond their own self-interest.

What does that look like?

Admitting you don't always have the answer is one example. What about taking credit for the wins and responsibility for the losses? Try flipping the usual script: give credit away to those who need it most (for example, to inspire or energise them) and accept responsibility yourself when things go wrong. Admitting you are wrong, asking peoples' opinion, not speaking first and longest in meetings. The list goes on.

What are some other ways that you can be humble in your daily leadership practice? See what happens.

NOT DOING

We're always doing. Planning, actioning, setting things in motion.

What about *not doing* today? Taking a step back, seeing the result of those plans that have been in motion. Take the time to think a bit more deeply. Just listen and observe.

What do you notice?

LESSONS LEARNED

L eaders take people on a journey. Yet one of the dangers of travel is that we don't often stop to see how far we have come. But when we do, it can help define more clearly where we're going and how we can get there.

In a busy working world, how do we incorporate the lessons from the things we do? Stress can be valuable—we learn, develop, remember—but this is only optimised if we follow stress with recovery.

Will you finish anything today? If not, are you close to the finish line? When you do finish consider the following:

- Clarify the project or task for which you want to capture the value of learning. When did it start? What was the initial scope and end result?
- Who was involved in making this happen? If you can, try to engage each person and get their reflections on the experience. Ask them, *What was more difficult? What came easy? What surprised you the most? What is a 'must' to replicate—or avoid—in the future?*
- Come together as a group to distil the main lessons learned and define actions for the future.

CHECKING IN WITHOUT CHECKING UP

What do your typical one-to-one interactions look like? Whether online or in person they may, at best, start with a few minutes of personal social chat before moving on to the work at hand. The status of things needing to be done. Then perhaps some of the personal stuff at the end or more likely just an agreement on next steps and a future check-in.

Sometimes, however, the greater impact that a leader can have is on the individual—the human being—regardless of any work needing to be completed at that time.

Who might be vulnerable right now? Perhaps a change in normal performance shows all is not well, or you learn of a difficult personal circumstance.

Checking in with that individual without mentioning any aspect of work is likely to be well received and may eventually create significant value for the work being done too.

Put people first today.

UPSKILLING (PART II)

The pandemic accelerated a conversation about the very human qualities that great leaders need. In my leadership workshops of the past several years, I've used a framework called the *Design Vowels* that enable a more human language of leadership to be practiced—Ambiguity, Empathy, Iteration, Observation, and Understanding. It also gets results.

Leading at distance—a rather common reality for post-pandemic teams—creates an extra layer of complexity and a unique set of challenges that requires new leadership skills. When visibility is decreased, so too awareness—the awareness that guides us and informs daily choices. Extra one-on-ones are often required, creating a heavier workload.

Asking other people more powerful questions is a good start. The typical *How are you?* will result in the usual *I'm fine,* which shows they're anything but.

Today, try asking questions that will tell you more. I've included a few below to get started. What others can you think of?

- What was the highlight of your week last week?
- What are you most looking forward to this week?
- Is there anything I can help you with today?

GIVE POWER AWAY

Inspiring others to action is one of the most important jobs for a leader.

In his bestselling book, *Drive*, Daniel Pink notes three factors that motivate people—autonomy, mastery and purpose.

When we have ownership of what we do, we naturally become more engaged. Empowering others is a hugely satisfying action for the leader too, since you see the results of that ownership in terms of development.

Empowerment was a cornerstone of the Humanizing Business initiative at SAP in Barcelona. Different work groups were given an allocated budget to personalise their workspace within the newly designed offices and some teams were even able to pick their own manager, incentivizing all team members to more fully collaborate and nudge them to treat everyone with respect. The overall aim was to bring decision-making power downwards.

What could *you* do to empower people? Perhaps rotate team leadership? Or when someone has a good idea, let them run with it?

How else could you give power away?

A SUBTLE DIFFERENCE
WITH A HUGE IMPACT

Do you have full autonomy on what you do today at work? How does that feel compared to when you are following someone else's instructions?

If you do lead others, give this a try:

Instead of telling people what to do, give them a problem to solve.

CHECKING THE TEMPERATURE

Pressure can serve a good purpose in making us perform. Too much however and it's counterproductive.

Part of the job of a leader is to gauge the pressure or *temperature* that people feel, and know the right setting for each individual to be their best and how that might be maintained in the longer term. It's important to note that this 'best' isn't simply performance, but also wellbeing.

Change is constant. Leaders must keep their hands on the temperature gauge and always be ready to adjust accordingly. For your own context, consider the following:

Signs that the temperature is too low (nothing gets done, too relaxed)

Actions to increase the temperature (e.g. a deadline or ambitious goal)

Signs that the temperature is too high (too much tension, poor balance)

Actions to decrease the temperature (e.g. company off-site, Friday afternoon celebration)

BELOW THE WATER-LINE

Teams and organisations, even people, can sometimes be viewed as an iceberg. What percentage of an iceberg is below the surface? On average, since ice has 9/10 of the density of water, 90% is submerged.

How do we move people and organisations?

We often focus on the visible metrics, policies and strategies. The things people say. These are the winds for our iceberg.

Yet, the greater force is the hidden currents, acting on the far greater mass that is below the water line. These are the habits, values, prejudice, and fears—the emotional rather than the rational. It is what people don't say.

The winds will continue to serve an important purpose in taking us where we want to go, but how might you tune in to those hidden currents?

SOCIAL MATTERS

Did 'virtual coffees' become more frequent for you during the global pandemic?

With everyone working at home, the social capital built up over years during countless coffee machine encounters likely began to erode. This was particularly troublesome for organisations that continued to recruit heavily—many teams were comprised of people who had known each other for years and others who had only ever been seen from the shoulders up. The complex dynamics at play provided many challenges for teams to keep doing good work.

We spend a lot of time with people at work, so it's probably best if we get along too. Ideally, we want to do (or make) better work but also make work better, as in a better experience. By considering the workplace a social community we improve both.

I talked to the leaders of several organisations during the pandemic whose young staff in particular were finding working from home difficult. This is primarily because all of their friendships were at work, so they weren't just missing office life but a social life too. Some even spent their own money to rent co-working space so they could spend their days together while the company office was locked down.

As a leader how can you help build social capital?

HELLO, THANK-YOU, GOOD MORNING

"Good manners are the lubricating oil of the organization."

Peter Drucker

I n *The Daily Stoic* Ryan Holiday and Stephen Hanselman present the example of the hiring practices of Walt Bettinger, the CEO of Charles Schwab.

Bettinger takes a job candidate to breakfast and asks the restaurant's manager to purposely mess up the candidate's breakfast order. He tests how they react. Do they get upset? Do they act rudely? Or do they treat the inconvenience with grace and kindness?

How employees treat each other is a key component of a healthy and positive culture. Don't just think about how the team talks to you, but to each other, especially those of lesser seniority. And the cleaning staff too. This will tell you a lot about the type of culture you have, and help create.

And don't forget about how you treat everyone else.

TRYING NEW THINGS

Danny MacAskill is an accomplished mountain biker from the Isle of Skye in Scotland. His speciality is trials biking—where the cyclist faces different obstacles without setting their feet on the ground. He frequently produces entertaining and inspiring video clips of his biking.

I'm one of his 1.8 million followers on Instagram. He is not only one of the world's best at what he does but also funny and humble. A hallmark of his videos is that he doesn't just show the perfect run or stunt, but all of the failed attempts that lead up to that one successful execution.

He is constantly trying new things, and that often means he falls of his bike. All he does is smile and go again.

One example in particular stands out for me.

He rode his bike across a metal chain that connects two blocks of concrete at a Blackpool beach. The chain is significantly narrower than the bike wheel and is perhaps four-five bike lengths. The total stunt lasts around ten seconds.

On the post description, MacAskill says he had been looking for the perfect chain since 2007 and that he had around 100 tries over two days before success.

One hundred tries!

Imagine how you'd feel on the 99th attempt. So much time and effort but no guarantee you'll pull it off.

Don't stop trying new things.

Create a culture where people feel they can keep trying too.

YOUR TEAM IDENTITY

When a football (or, soccer for US readers) team has a new manager in Europe there is the usual talk of the manager making the team 'theirs'.

In the highly pressurised world of sport results, this can relate to buying some time, or convincing the club directors to finance the purchase of better players, but the issue of identity is important.

A new manager will inherit the players who were at the club before they arrived—those led by the previous manager. They usually want to bring players who they know or admire. Then they get the team to play in the style (including tactics and formation) they believe will get results.

What about your team? What is their unique identity? Are you happy with the way they 'play' to get the best results?

Take some time to define the habits, norms, rituals, and values most appropriate for the team. Involve the team in the process too.

A DELICATE BALANCE

L eadership needs energy!

And the style of leadership required today is especially exhausting. Leading at distance means working harder, with more issues arising from a new working context and the difficulty of resolving conflict when not face-to-face. More individual interactions are needed and this human dimension takes both time and significant emotional energy.

I've coached some highly empathetic leaders who were close to burnout. It takes significant effort to partake in active listening, a coaching mindset, and simply having a deeper understanding of another human being. Now multiply that by the headcount some leaders have in their team.

Empathy can be painful—literally. Some hyper-empathetic people may produce the stress hormone cortisol when engaging closely with the problems of another person and some even have mirror neurons that actually create the same feeling in them that the other person is experiencing.

You can't give everything away.

How do you balance being a caring leader while retaining energy and space for you and your family?

NOVEMBER 27TH

THE VIEW FROM
THE BALCONY

'm a keen observer of sport, particularly how athletes are coached. In football, during a game, coaches are on the touchline. They are seen by their team, can shout instructions and have a direct line of contact to their charges. They're close to the action.

Sometimes a coach is cast from the touchline for unruly behaviour. They then have to watch the action unfold from the stadium seating higher up. They can't engage directly, but they do have a better view. A different perspective. They can see the broad sweep of play and not just specific zones. Some coaches even find they prefer to be there.

Sometimes we're on the field of play, in the middle of the action. We can direct what's going on.

Sometimes we're higher up. On the balcony. Gaining perspective.

What's the view from the balcony today?

LEADERSHIP   361

THE VIEW FROM
THE BALCONY

'm a keen observer of sport, particularly how athletes are coached. In football, during a game, coaches are on the touchline. They are seen by their team, can shout instructions and have a direct line of contact to their charges. They're close to the action.

Sometimes a coach is cast from the touchline for unruly behaviour. They then have to watch the action unfold from the stadium seating higher up. They can't engage directly, but they do have a better view. A different perspective. They can see the broad sweep of play and not just specific zones. Some coaches even find they prefer to be there.

Sometimes we're on the field of play, in the middle of the action. We can direct what's going on.

Sometimes we're higher up. On the balcony. Gaining perspective.

What's the view from the balcony today?

GET INTO THE FIELD

W hen I was a young innovation consultant, I spent some
time doing ethnographic field research in Mexico.
As part of a new marketing campaign for a major
multi-national, I conducted *shadowing* work across four major cities. I went into the homes of our marketing targets with my video
camera and followed them during their normal day, including
picking kids up from school and going to the supermarket.

The logic is that we learn much more about people and their
needs when we see them in their natural environment. By observing and asking powerful questions, we can dig to a deeper level of
insight that is not as available to us in an office-based work environment where bias and assumptions prevail.

It reminds me of a cartoon by Tom Fishburne in the book
Talking to Humans. There are three men in an office, filled with
computers, pizza, and post-it notes. One says:

"If I were our teenage girl target, I would love our new product.

The other asks; "Have you actually talked to any to make sure?"

The third chips in, "What? And leave this room?"

What are the assumptions you need to challenge in order to move
forward?

A one-minute observation may beat a 1,000-page report.

How can you get out of the office and into the field?

YOU'RE ALLOWED TO CHANGE YOUR MIND

When was the last time you changed your mind about something?

Sometimes you might feel tied to a position or belief because you have made it public. Leaders are often more visible than other people, and their opinions too. Yet in a world of rapid change, where new information and facts constantly present themselves, it won't help to stubbornly stick to an outdated belief.

Instead, have the confidence to change your mind, and know why you did so.

The approach may be linked to a decision-making framework called 'Strong Opinions, Weakly Held' by Stanford University Professor Paul Saffo that involves making an early conclusion or hypothesis and then actively trying to prove it wrong. Look for data that doesn't fit and share the conclusion early with others to see how they react.

What new information has come to light that means some of your current beliefs or opinions are outdated? It doesn't matter how long you've had them.

FINDING THE RIGHT QUESTIONS

L eadership is not about finding the right answers.

It's about finding the right questions to answer.

This is true in the coaching process and how we develop other people. There is significantly more value in someone working something out for themselves, guided by your questions, than you simply giving them the answer.

This is also true of the work we do. If we can hold back from the rapid definition of a problem, we might be able to open up new and fresh possibilities—rather than simply copy and paste what has been done before. Diagnosing and re-framing the problem ought to be the focus instead of jumping to the solution.

Defining the right question is often more difficult than finding the right answer.

Don't jump to action today and think it's the same problem as before. You might get stuck.

NOTES ON YOUR JOURNEY THROUGH
LEADERSHIP IN NOVEMBER:

DECEMBER

COMMUNITY

WHAT THE HELL IS WATER?

D avid Foster Wallace was an accomplished writer and University professor. In his Commencement address to the 2005 class at Kenyon College, he opened with a story of two goldfish swimming along when one day they encounter another, older fish swimming in the opposite direction. The older fish says, 'Morning boys, how's the water?' The two younger fish then look at each other and say, 'What the hell is water?'

I use this story in many of my classes. On the simplest level, it highlights the power of awareness. There are countless stories of people dying who begin to see the world around them much more vividly. Don't wait till then.

As we near the end of another year, it might be worthwhile to remember, and appreciate, the miracle of life, and all that surrounds us. Maybe even say to ourselves, as Foster Wallace remarks at the end of his address. 'This is water, this is water'.

[YOUR JOURNAL]

WELLBEING DOESN'T EXIST IN ISOLATION

Wellbeing is a journey that starts with the self but involves others. Our families, co-workers, friends, neighbours, and really any and all beings (indeed every natural element) with whom we share the planet Earth, are all, at some point, part of our journey.

Many wellbeing models and definitions, including those from the World Health Organization and OECD (Organisation for Economic Co-operation and Development), make this eco-system explicit by highlighting the importance of *social wellbeing*.

Wherever you are on your own wellbeing journey, how you connect with others will impact where you go and the speed at which you travel.

Who is part of your wellbeing community? How will you connect with them today?

COMMUNITY COHESION

The work of academics Zunin and Myers on the emotional highs and lows that follow a natural disaster, such as an earthquake or tsunami, made a comeback during the pandemic. Their reflections show that most of the positive initial phases are supported by community.

They describe an initial heroic phase which is followed by a period of community cohesion. People come together to face the trauma and this act shows the best of human nature.

Think today about how your own community (at work, home, neighbourhood, or social networks) may have rallied together in recent times. If that is not immediately apparent, think about any small signs of collective positivity that you can build on through your own actions.

Hold close to a central idea: by building on the notions of community, what is the new reality that we can build together?

WORLD HAPPINESS IN 2020

hat do you think the results were of the World Happiness Report in the year everything changed? It's not as bad as you may think—because of community.

A publication of the UN's Sustainable Development Solutions Network, powered by data from Gallup and Lloyd's, the report is co-written by experts worldwide and has, since 2012, found the Nordic countries to be the happiest in the world.

The 2020 report showed that trust and generosity helped us weather the storm. The pandemic provided the opportunity to see the kindness of other people. The material effects of the crisis were undoubted—including uncertainty around income, employment, health, and social connection. Yet seeing the best of us rise up helped to offset this damage, and inspire us to act.

Look around you today to see the kindness of others.

CONNECTING IN A DISCONNECTED WORLD

When I think back on those early weeks of the pandemic, I'm always surprised by the contrast in my social life... Like many other aspects of our lives today, 'socialising' during lockdowns and pandemic restrictions was done via video and an endless stream of virtual coffees, happy hours, quizzes, and family gatherings on Zoom. I actually heard from some people for the first time in years and I spoke to my mum on the most regular basis since I had moved to Spain in 2003.

Restrictions are lessening thankfully, but as we contemplate a future that may be disconnected on some levels forever, or at least subject to disruption and change, how can we stay connected?

Note down below your own experiences on staying in touch (or getting back into touch) with people throughout the pandemic. Are you still at it? What intentions to connect might you commit to going forward?

HOW CAN I HELP?

I know you're busy. At home, at work, in between. But try this and see how it goes:

Ask someone if they need any help today.

VOLUNTEERING AND MENTAL HEALTH

The pandemic gave rise to a volunteer army of millions around the world. Numerous studies show that volunteering results in better mental and physical health, life satisfaction, self-esteem, happiness, and lower levels of depression and psychological distress.

From picking up groceries and other essentials for neighbours to donating to foodbanks and participating in vaccine trials, people felt good through doing good. More than twelve million people in the UK alone volunteered during 2020, one third for the first time, and most planned to continue doing so. Business has seen the value of this movement and many companies now offer their employees the freedom and flexibility to contribute to a cause, thereby energizing them and convincing their best talent that they can find purpose while at work.

Is there any aspect of volunteering that you can get involved in today?

PUT YOUR HANDS TOGETHER

As far as I'm aware, it started in Italy. It then became a nightly ritual soon after around my home in Barcelona. I was also very aware of the same nightly practice across the UK. I'm sure it happened in many other countries around the world too.

The daily show of appreciation for the superheroes of healthcare during those first terrifying months of the pandemic served as a pressure release valve. The horrors of the day—as we saw images of Intensive Care Units bursting at the seams, people gasping for breath and healthcare workers woefully under protected by a lack of Personal Protection Equipment—were salved at night as we came together to applaud and make noise.

How might you show appreciation for others today? Maybe it's just saying thank you. It makes a difference.

BARRIO

*B*arrio is the Spanish word for neighbourhood.

Growing up in a small town in the West of Scotland, I remember a very close-knit community. Doors were always unlocked and neighbours would frequently 'pop-in' for a chat or a cup of tea. There was a summer fair in town every year. Is this just a feature of a bygone age or might we open up more to people around us?

I love living in Barcelona—and one of its distinct features as a city is the different neighbourhoods, from *Gracia* to *Eixample* and *Les Corts*, which all have a unique personality. In fact, each place that I have lived previously has had its own set of features that make me feel at home.

Studies show that our social wellbeing doesn't just depend on contact with close friends and family, but also the fleeting interactions with people in our daily lives. Maybe we don't always know their name but the hello, goodbye, wave and other pleasantries to the lady at the school gates, the doorman, the man in the coffee shop—all make a difference to our wellbeing, as well as theirs. These interactions keep a community strong.

Think about your own *barrio* today. Let yourself engage with it.

THE NEXT GLOBAL PANDEMIC

The previous century's flu pandemic lasted until 1920, but there was a spike in suicides the following year, in 1921.

For many just getting through the worst days of the pandemic took all their energy. As the world begins to put the pieces together again, much has been made of the fact that the dangers of stress, anxiety, and depression could follow on the heels of COVID-19 as the next global pandemic.

I believe loneliness might be the even bigger danger. Societal and demographic shifts over the past few decades have meant this has been a growing danger. It has been well documented that an increasing amount of older people might go weeks without talking to another human being. The pandemic also gave rise to an increasing number of young adults who suffered from social isolation.

I think there's an opportunity here. The anxiety that many will feel re-starting their post-pandemic lives may allow them to empathise with those who have suffered from loneliness for a long time. Talking to them will facilitate a sense of distance from their own worries and perhaps help them realise things aren't as bad as they might think.

Is there someone in your life, an older person perhaps, who might be lonely? Spending even a small amount of time with them, or simply checking in with a phone call, will do you both a world of good.

THE HUNGER AND PAIN OF SOCIAL ISOLATION

The pandemic highlighted the social nature, and needs, of all human beings.

Research from the Massachusetts Institute of Technology found that we crave interactions in the same region of our brains that we crave food. A related study showed we experience social exclusion in the same region of our brain that we experience physical pain.

Other research by the University of New South Wales found that, after periods of social isolation, the introduction of social interaction had the effect of reducing cravings for food and nicotine.

We need each other, not just for overall wellbeing, but for good brain and behavioural health too.

CONNECT TO GROW

Networking has long been a valuable part of a professional life. Maybe you think you're an accomplished networker or maybe it's something that makes you feel uncomfortable. In any case, it comes with a variety of benefits, allowing us to learn, recognise our blind spots, and inspire us to action. Think about the following steps today:

Reflect on your existing network
Who are the people that have the biggest influence on your own thinking and development?

Think on gaps you might want to address
What else are you curious or passionate about? What trends—inside and/or outside your own domain—would you like to build knowledge in?

Become a seeker
Connect with people who are *the opposite to you*. Find them within and outside of your organisation, in your same and different functions. Think of varying levels of experience.

Build new relationships
Be brave. Make an introduction! Not everyone (especially those external to your own company) will be receptive, but that doesn't matter.

Engage with your network on an ongoing basis
Have conversations with close relationships. Add to an online discussion or share a post with a more distant one. Become an active member of your community.

THE NEW OLYMPIC MOTTO

The delayed Tokyo 2020 Olympics were, all things considered, a success.

As the delayed start date of the Games approached in late July of 2021, with the city of Tokyo still gripped with the worst effects of the COVID-19 virus, there was increasing pressure to cancel them altogether.

The organisers persisted, safe in the belief, I think, that the world wanted to come together again. As many of us remained confined on some level, seeing any signs of togetherness was appealing.

In the opening address Thomas Bach, the International Olympic Committee president shared the new Olympic motto: *Higher, Faster, Stronger—Together.*

He talked about the unifying power of sport but I think it's more than that. It's a powerful reminder that we become better versions of ourselves when we connect with others.

THE SOCIAL NETWORK

When I first moved to Spain in 2003 at the age of 25, I lost contact with a good number of friends. Indeed, I've often reflected on the sacrifice I made in making the move—your mid 20s are, after all, a time in your life that is highly social and potentially, a lot of fun.

During those early years, as I moved from one temporary apartment to another, I'd go to an Internet café to email. I used phone cards to phone home. Online newspapers and other news outlets were rudimentary. I felt the distance. I almost moved back home on a number of occasions.

The Big Tech explosion helped significantly. Social networks and smartphones made me feel closer to home and today I enjoy a number of rich friendships with people I rarely see face-to-face.

What I want to highlight here is the good in technology and social networks at a time when it is being lambasted from all sides.

Yes, it has been designed to be highly exploitative and addictive, but with some practice, you can get the best out of it.

How can you do that exactly? It's not an easy question to answer, but it's worth trying. Maybe start by thinking about the positive attributes, for example the way it helps you connect with loved ones, and make full use of that.

BIG TECH IS CHANGING

We've all experienced it. We check our phone or email, or open a social media application. We get a micro-dose of dopamine, the reward hormone which plays a role in many forms of addiction.

Big Tech designers have played on the brain function associated with dopamine, with features such as notifications appearing after a short delay (likened by some as playing a slot machine) in order to maximize the brain's anticipation and levels of dopamine.

The Center for Humane Technology, a US-based think tank comprised of former Big Tech employees, believes we are in a "race to the bottom of the brain stem to extract human attention." Their work focuses on actions to reverse *human downgrading* and help drive a new generation of humane technology that embraces human nature.

I do see signs of change.

It used to be that if the application was free, you were the product and companies harvested your precious data to generate marketing insights that allowed them to make billions in revenue.

Now, users are being empowered and new technology companies see that opportunity. In mid-2021, *The Economist* reported on the new rules of the creator economy whereby content creators are starting to monetize what they do and what they create.

Don't automatically give your data and content away for free today. Check for alternatives and let's create a more positive technology landscape together.

CHECK YOUR PRIVILEGE

'm very aware of my privilege.

It wasn't always the case but in the past few years I've recognised my advantage. I'm a white man, for starters. My native language is English and I'm European. I'm part of a minority in other areas of my life but these four characteristics are enough to give me a natural advantage over most of the world's population.

As you go through your day today and interact with those around you, ask yourself if you enjoy any sort of privilege over others.

It might just help make what you do and what you say more appropriate. And make us all happier.

YOU ARE NOT THE CENTRE OF THE UNIVERSE

Human beings, all 7.6 billion of us, make up just 0.01% of all living things on planet Earth.

Bacteria make up 13%. All other creatures, from insects to fungi, fish and animals, make up 5%. Plants are the dominant part of the Earth's biomass, making up 82%.

0.01%. Yet we have caused the loss of 83% of all wild mammals and half of plants.

Attitudes are changing, thankfully. For example, new laws in the UK formally recognise animals as sentient beings and take into account the fact that animals are capable of experiencing emotions such as pain and joy.

But we need to go farther and faster in recognising that we share this world. This isn't just good for the planet and our communities, it's good for us as individuals. When we stop acting as if our immediate needs are the most important thing, we become less stressed, less anxious, more patient and understanding, and better able to see the wonder of the world around us.

We can learn to enjoy the ride more instead of trying to steer every moment of it.

UFOs ARE BILLIONAIRES FROM ANOTHER PLANET

I n the summer of 2021 as Richard Branson and Jeff Bezos travelled away from the Earth to herald the start of the space tourism industry, a viral joke circulated the Internet that UFOs were in fact billionaires from other planets.

It's a funny line that nonetheless makes you think. If beings from another planet did come to visit us, what would they see? What would they think?

There is a wide variety in the views of what Branson and Bezos have done by travelling into space, from it being pioneering innovations to simple vanity projects. One train of thought caught my attention regarding the money spent, which, if used in other areas could have solved problems that have been around for generations regarding education, health and nutrition.

For the rest of us, even though we don't have the money to travel into space, it is still worth considering how might we direct our resources and energy to improve our corner of the world. Start with your immediate community.

A QUESTION OF DEGREES

I t's likely that the climate crisis will represent the biggest issue of our lifetime. And that of our children too.

The first major review of the climate science since 2013, the 2021 IPCC report—the United Nations special advisory—made headlines around the world for highlighting the scale of the problems we face. The report authors noted that it is a "code red" for humanity. On the simplest level it's a question of degrees:

1.5°C
A rise of 1.5 versus pre-industrial levels has long held as the outer limit of safety for us all, and on which many international targets and agreements have been based. The report states we are already at a rise of 1.1 and are likely to breach 1.5 by the mid 2030s or earlier unless more drastic action is taken now.

2°C
This half-degree difference is significant and marks the different between changes which might be reversed (though admittedly over decades and longer) past a tipping point of irreversible damage. Fires and floods would become an even more common occurrence, sea levels would rise 3m instead of 0.5m, submerging areas where millions currently live, and up to a fifth of insects would lose their habitat affecting pollination and the wider ecosystem.

Half a degree. A tiny difference with enormous impact. Your own tiny actions, each day, can also have an enormous impact.

A SUSTAINABLE WORLD NEEDS SUSTAINABLE PEOPLE

W hat does sustainability mean?

It's about something that *lasts,* right? And don't we all want things to last as long as possible? Our happiness, our lives, our success, our friendships… the list goes on.

I want to highlight that sustainability isn't just about environmental care—it's about making it possible for all of us to live a long and happy life.

And this sustainability is connected across all levels—us as individuals, our teams and communities, the world.

Leading a sustainable life is not necessarily about living a life of compromise. It is living a life of abundance!

MOVE THE DATE

T he March 2020 lockdown that took place in many countries around the world gave rise to some interesting phenomena. After just a few weeks, the canals in Venice started running cleaner water. It was possible to see the Himalayas from certain parts of India for the first time in more than 30 years. And the *earth overshoot day* enjoyed a significant improvement for the first time in decades.

Earth Overshoot Day marks the date when humanity's demand for ecological resources and services in a given year exceeds what the planet can regenerate for that year. It is calculated by the Global Footprint Network, an international research organization.

In 2021, Earth Overshoot Day was July 29ᵗʰ. When the analysis first began in 1970, the overshoot date was December 30ᵗʰ.

Nature has shown its impressive ability to bounce back, but it won't always be able to do it without our help.

SHAPE THE WORLD

I t's easy to feel powerless in the face of the enormous challenge that is the world's climate change crisis. And powerlessness can lead to inactivity.

Yet, I truly believe we can all play an active part in the new post-pandemic world rather than be passive passengers. There is a huge opportunity from the pandemic in terms of the mindset reset we have all experienced—so we can build a better world and a happier life.

One example of individual habits driving large-scale change during the pandemic was the increase in walking. This provided the necessary nudge for cities worldwide, including Milan and Paris, to accelerate the re-design of their urban centres to be more friendly for walkers and cyclists, and less welcoming of cars.

Two of the biggest climate impacts we cause, especially in the rich world, is how we eat and how we move. Just by considering the following you can start to make a difference (but don't stop here).

- What's for dinner today? Plant-based diets can reduce emissions by up to 50% compared to the average emission intensive western diet. I'm not preaching for veganism necessarily but do you need to eat meat *every* day?
- How many short trips will you make today? Walk instead of driving, or at least consider public transport. You'll save money, contribute to cleaner air, get more fit, feel less frustrated, and think more clearly.

THE URBAN RESET

T he famous octagonal block design of the Barcelona *Eixample* district was an effort to free the city from the confines of the suffocating medieval walls where life expectancy during the industrial revolution was as low as 23 years. Ildefons Cerdà designed the blocks in 1859 as a means of improving sustainability and quality of life. He was an incredible visionary and even conceived of the chamfered corners of the blocks so people could see around corners as he envisioned some form of motorised transport.

It was a shame that the trajectory of 20th century growth turned his green vision into the likes of any other city with huge volumes of traffic and the interior spaces of the blocks—the green space that he envisaged for neighbours to use to come together became no more than carparks.

But I think he would be encouraged by the reset caused by the pandemic and the bold moves currently being made by the city administration.

Since March 2020, the city has reclaimed around 80,000m^2 of the city from motor vehicles, transforming it into sidewalks, playgrounds, bike lanes, and restaurant terraces. It's now much more pleasant to walk, live, and work in the city centre. Indeed, it encourages you to stick around rather than escape and it reminds me of the initial attraction I had to living in a city in the first place.

The overall plan is to convert 21 streets, totalling 33 km (around 20 miles), into pedestrian green spaces. In total, a third of all the streets in the Eixample will be transformed into a so-called pedestrian green axis by 2030.

That's an inspiring urban reset.

GET DOWN THE LOCAL

The traditional British pub has been disappearing over the past few decades and this change is affecting the fabric of community as well as the health of the people in it.

University of Oxford research looked at the benefits of old-style community pubs relative to the high street bars that have come to dominate in recent years. They found that people who had a "local" that they patronised regularly had more close friends, felt happier, were more satisfied with their lives, more embedded into their local communities, and more trusting of those around them. They also found that an evening meal, with alcohol, had these same effects. Of the many social activities that trigger the endorphin system in humans (including laughter, singing and exercise), the consumption of alcohol seems to be one of the most effective.

Some anthropologists trace this back to our ancestors' time around the campfire, where few activities were possible other than eating, drinking and socialising.

Even current day bushmen in South Africa have been found to talk of boring factual topics during the day with evening conversations focused on social topics, storytelling and jokes.

To build your community and improve your social wellbeing, you know what to do (so long as your personal situation allows it).

Go to the local pub.

At night.

And drink some alcohol.

GIVING IS BETTER THAN RECEIVING

t's a wonderful thing when we receive a gift. The object itself might be special and the fact that someone was thinking of you too.

But do you also find that giving a gift can be even more special?

It's the reciprocity that builds community and our social wellbeing.

STAKEHOLDERS OVER SHAREHOLDERS

I n October 2019, Marc Benioff, the co-founder and CEO of Salesforce, wrote an op-ed article in *The New York Times* arguing for a change in the way business is conducted.

At the core of his plea was a call for business to take a more active role in the problems faced by society and to think about stakeholders rather than just shareholders.

Shareholders have a direct financial interest in the success of a company. The capitalist system is based on generating a sustainable return on the investment that shareholders make.

Stakeholders are any party that are affected by the actions of a company. For example, the local community where a company is headquartered or the employees who work there.

Shareholders are always stakeholders, but stakeholders are not always shareholders.

Might you broaden your own perspective today on who is affected by your actions rather than just consider those who have a direct interest in your doing well?

VALUE(S)

Sustainability is most often viewed in terms of the environment.

Yet it is also viewed in terms of how long a company can remain competitive—that is the sustainable advantage that a company has in the market. And this is no easy task. The average age of the Fortune 500 (the largest companies in the US) was 60 years in 1960 and less than 18 years today.

How do companies maintain a competitive position? By building a strong culture that innovates on a regular basis, by taking care of all stakeholders, and by operating based on a set of core values. This is the path to long-term success.

Business is focused on generating value, and they have the best chance of doing that in the long term if they have a strong base of working founded on strong values.

Does your company follow such an approach? Do you?

BUSINESS AND SOCIETY

T he close role of business in society espoused by Salesforce's Marc Benioff is not a new idea. In the late 1780s, the New Lanark cotton mills in Central Scotland was one of the first examples of business looking after the interest of stakeholders.

Mill manager Robert Owen transformed the lives of the 2,000 people who lived and worked there, including 500 children—all while delivering commercial success. Many leading royals, statesmen, and reformers from around Europe visited the mills to find a clean and healthy environment with a happy workforce that did not compromise a prosperous business.

I was born a little further west from the mills and grew up as the famous Ravenscraig steelworks became one of the largest producers of steel in the world in the 1980s. Its closure in 1992 affected thousands and greatly impacted the local community.

We went backwards.

Can we now go forwards? I think there's signs that it's possible. Purpose found in and out of the office, passion, a greater awareness of the world around us, the importance of human leadership and empathy at work, and many more themes we've discussed throughout the year give me optimism that the future relationship of business and society is a bright one.

STRONGER PEOPLE, STRONGER SOCIETY

Arla Foods is a Danish multinational cooperative and the largest producer of dairy products in Scandinavia. They are a highly successful company that enjoyed a record year in 2020. They had a natural advantage being a food company, but they are also a strong community. They look after their people—their employees of course but also all stakeholders across the supply chain. This makes good business sense and allows for a long-term view.

The company's new strategy combines employee wellbeing and Corporate Social Responsibility—called *Stronger People, Stronger Society*—and shows the close links, as well as potential, of both.

Shouldn't we all be similarly inspired when we go to work each day? Does community exist at your place of work?

DUTY DU JOUR

We're almost at the end of another calendar year. Whether you've just picked up *The Daily Reset* or you've been following the entries all year, I hope you understand the importance of today. Just like every day.

Your life journey, and this year's journey, is made of *jours*—days.

You have a duty, as we all do, to do your bit to make this world a better place.

That starts with your community.

Maybe you can join a local volunteer initiative—micro groups have sprung up around the UK planting pollinator-friendly plants, running weekly litter picks, lobbying local supermarkets to reduce waste—or start one yourself.

THE DAILY RESET

A t the end of today, you'll go to sleep. Well, probably tomorrow morning.

Each time you do, you have a chance to reset. Perhaps you've had a great day, maybe a terrible one. But at the end of each comes the chance to reset and start again.

As you get ready to start another new year, another chance to reset, please remember that the means to do so is in the small reset that we have the privilege to experience each and every day of our lives.

I'd like to finish this year of nudges with some words from Rabbie Burns, the Scottish poet. There's a chance you'll sing, or at least hear these words of 'Auld Lang Syne' or 'days gone by' in the coming hours. Reflect on the days gone by this year, of the kindness of your acquaintances, or community, this month.

Reflect, then reset.

Thank-you.

Should auld acquaintance be forgot
And never brought to mind?
Should auld acquaintance be forgot
And days of auld lang syne?

For auld lang syne, my dear
For auld lang syne
We'll tak a cup o' kindness yet
For days of auld lang syne.

NOTES ON YOUR JOURNEY THIS YEAR:

NOTES ON YOUR JOURNEY THIS YEAR:

NOTES ON YOUR JOURNEY THIS YEAR:

ALSO BY STEVEN P. MACGREGOR

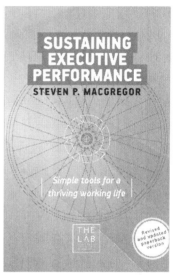

WWW.STEVENMACGREGOR.COM

🐦 @spmacg 📷 @spmacg
💼 Dr. Steven MacGregor

VISIT **WWW.DAILYRESET.ME** FOR EXTRA RESOURCES

Printed in Great Britain
by Amazon